Progressive Farmer®
COUNTRY PLACE
COOKBOOK

D1431410

Designed by LuAnn Smith

Edited by Carolyn Garrick Stern

Recipes compiled by Nancy Stuart

Progressive Farmer, Inc.
Birmingham, Alabama 35209

PRODUCTS DIVISION

©1993 by Progressive Farmer, Inc.
Manufactured in the United States of America
Library of Congress Catalog Card Number: 93-085798
International Standard Book Number: 0-8487-1422-9

❖

Table of Contents

Preface

For more than 100 years, *Progressive Farmer* has been a member of the household. A large part of our involvement has been in presenting delicious, nutritious recipes.

Every year, we receive hundreds of suggestions for dishes from our readers. Home economists in our test kitchens check them for accuracy and reliability, and we choose the best to publish in our magazine.

In the *Progressive Farmer Country Place Cookbook,* we present the best of the best — recipes that stood out at the top of their categories. And we've included a wide variety of dishes so you'll find just the right one for a quick family meal or a special celebration.

We've done our best to make this book easy to use. In most cases, the recipes are complete on one page. However, some were just too good to restrict or pass up so we've allowed more space.

There are notes about nutritional content when a dish is especially healthy, and some alternative cooking tips have been added. We've also included some of the recipes that nourished us in the earlier years of this century — our "Vintage Recipes."

Also, we've found that people love to talk about food. Taking a hint from our popular "Cornerstones" page of quotations, we share some comments about the glories of the table throughout the book.

So gather up the best and freshest ingredients you can find and create your own culinary masterpiece. Enjoy!

Appetizers
Beverages & Snacks

PROGRESSIVE FARMER
DECEMBER 1942

TOMATO JUICE COCKTAIL

Combine 1 quart canned tomato juice, 1 teaspoon sugar, juice of 1 lemon, ½ cup kraut juice, and ¼ teaspoon grated horseradish or ½ teaspoon chili sauce. Add salt and pepper to taste.

PROGRESSIVE FARMER
JANUARY 1932

BAKED CHEESE FONDUE

Scald 1 cup milk and pour over 1 cup soft breadcrumbs. Add 1 tablespoon fat, 1 cup grated cheese, and salt to taste. Beat 3 egg yolks lightly and add to the mixture. Then fold in stiffly beaten egg whites.

Turn into a greased baking dish, set into a pan of hot water, and bake in a moderate oven (350°) until firm.

Spicy Vegetable Dip

1   cup small-curd cottage cheese
1   cup plain low-fat yogurt
2   teaspoons lemon juice
⅛   teaspoon hot sauce
1   (0.6-ounce) package Italian salad dressing mix

    Combine all ingredients in container of an electric blender; process until smooth.
    Serve with fresh vegetables. Yield: 2 cups.

Dill Dip

1   (8-ounce) package cream cheese, softened
½   cup sour cream
½   cup mayonnaise
1   tablespoon minced onion
1   tablespoon minced fresh parsley
2   teaspoons dried dillweed

    Combine all ingredients in container of an electric blender; process until smooth. Cover and chill.
    Serve with fresh vegetables. Yield: 2 cups.

FREDA HOLMES, Oklahoma City, Okla.

> *"We may live without friends; we may live without books; but civilized man cannot live without cooks."*
>
> OWEN MEREDITH

Cheese Straws

¾   cup butter or margarine, softened
1   (5-ounce) jar sharp process cheese spread
2¼   cups all-purpose flour
1   teaspoon ground red pepper

Combine butter and cheese in a large mixing bowl; beat well at medium speed with an electric mixer. Combine flour and pepper; gradually add to cheese mixture, mixing until dough is no longer crumbly. Shape mixture into a ball.

Use a cookie gun to shape dough into straws, following manufacturer's instructions. Place on ungreased baking sheets and cut at 2-inch intervals.

Bake at 375° for 13 to 15 minutes or until lightly browned. Store in airtight containers, placing wax paper between layers. Yield: 7 dozen.

NIDA O. DEWBERRY, Shelby, N.C.

Mexican Hot Sauce

4   medium tomatoes, peeled and quartered
1   medium onion, quartered
1   clove garlic, halved
1   teaspoon red pepper flakes
1   tablespoon chili powder
1   teaspoon salt
¼   teaspoon sugar
1   tablespoon vegetable oil

Position knife blade in food processor bowl; add first 7 ingredients. Process until smooth.

Combine tomato mixture and oil in a saucepan; bring to a boil. Reduce heat and simmer, uncovered, 5 minutes, stirring occasionally. Yield: about 2¼ cups.

MARY BAIRD, Long Lane, Mo.

Cashew Chicken Fingers

1	cup coarsely ground cashews
1	cup soft breadcrumbs
4	egg whites
½	cup cornstarch
2	teaspoons salt
2	teaspoons sugar
¼	cup dry sherry
4	chicken breast halves, skinned, boned, and cut into 3-inch strips

Vegetable oil

Combine cashews and breadcrumbs; set aside. Beat egg whites at medium speed with an electric mixer just until blended. Combine cornstarch, salt, and sugar; stir into egg whites. Add sherry, stirring until well mixed.

Dredge chicken pieces in crumb mixture; dip in egg-white mixture and dredge again in crumb mixture.

Pour oil to depth of 3 inches into a Dutch oven; heat to 375°. Fry chicken pieces in hot oil about 2 minutes on each side; drain on paper towels.

Yield: 4 servings.

CAROL DWYER, Meeker, Okla.

> *"The cherry tomato is a marvelous invention, producing as it does a satisfactory explosive squish when bitten."*
>
> *JUDITH MARTIN (MISS MANNERS)*

Ground Beef Dip

1   pound ground beef
½   medium onion, chopped
1   cup canned whole tomatoes, undrained and
        chopped
2½   tablespoons jalapeño relish
1   (8-ounce) loaf process cheese spread
1   (8-ounce) loaf process cheese spread with
        jalapeño

Cook ground beef and onion in a large skillet over medium heat until meat is browned, stirring to crumble; drain. Wipe pan drippings from skillet.

Return beef mixture to skillet; stir in tomatoes and remaining ingredients. Cook over low heat, stirring constantly, until cheese melts. Serve with corn chips.

Yield: 4 cups.

JENNIFER C. CLAXTON, Vidalia, Ga.

Hot Artichoke Spread

1   (14-ounce) can artichokes, drained and chopped
1   cup mayonnaise
½   cup grated Parmesan cheese
¼   teaspoon pepper

Combine all ingredients in a 1-quart casserole. Microwave at MEDIUM (50% power) 3 to 4 minutes, stirring every minute. Serve with crackers. Yield: about 1½ cups.

Note: Spread may be baked in a conventional oven at 350° for 20 minutes.

JUANITA SMITH, Atmore, Ala.

Orange Slush Punch

2   cups sugar
6   cups water
4   bananas, mashed
½   cup lemon juice
2   (12-ounce) cans frozen orange juice concentrate,
      thawed and undiluted
1   (46-ounce) can pineapple juice
1   (67.6-ounce) bottle lemon-lime carbonated
      beverage, chilled

Combine sugar and water in a Dutch oven; cook over high heat, stirring often, until sugar dissolves. Let cool. Stir in banana and next 3 ingredients. Freeze until firm.

Remove from freezer about 2 hours before serving. Break frozen mixture into large pieces and place in punch bowl. Pour in carbonated beverage; stir gently until slushy.

Yield: 6½ quarts.

BILLIE JO WORKING, Dallas, Ga.

Spiced Tea Mix

1   cup sugar
½   cup instant tea
½   cup orange-flavored breakfast beverage crystals
2   (0.28-ounce) envelopes unsweetened
      lemon-flavored drink mix
1   teaspoon pumpkin pie spice
1   teaspoon dried lemon peel

Combine all ingredients. Store in an airtight container. To serve, stir 1 tablespoon mix into ½ cup hot water. Yield: 1½ cups tea mix.

NONA WILSON, Vernon, Tex.

Hot Cranberry Drink

3   quarts water
3   cups fresh cranberries
3   lemons, sliced
3   oranges, sliced
12   whole cloves
3   (2-inch) sticks cinnamon
2   cups honey
1   teaspoon ground nutmeg

Combine first 4 ingredients in a Dutch oven; bring to a boil. Cook 7 to 10 minutes or until cranberry skins pop. Strain mixture.

Place cloves and cinnamon in center of a small square of cheesecloth; tie with string. Combine spice bag, strained liquid, honey, and nutmeg in a Dutch oven. Cook over medium heat 10 minutes, stirring occasionally. Remove spice bag. Serve hot.

Yield: 3½ quarts.

SCINTILLA COFFMAN, Tucson, Ariz.

Hot Cocoa Mix

10⅔ cups instant nonfat dry milk powder
1   (16-ounce) container instant cocoa mix for milk
1   (16-ounce) package powdered sugar, sifted
1   (6-ounce) jar nondairy coffee creamer
½   teaspoon salt

Combine all ingredients. Store in an airtight container. To serve, place ⅓ cup mix in a cup. Add 1 cup boiling water and stir well.

Yield: 16 cups mix (48 servings).

MRS. WILLIAM YODER, JR., Montezuma, Ga.

Holiday Confetti Mix

1   (16-ounce) package candy-coated chocolate
        pieces
1   (16-ounce) package candy-coated peanut pieces
1   (15-ounce) package raisins
1   (12-ounce) package butterscotch morsels
1   (12-ounce) can mixed nuts

Combine all ingredients and store in airtight containers in a cool, dry place. Yield: 11 cups.

BILLIE BLANTON, Kingsport, Tenn.

Granola Mix

5   cups regular oats, uncooked
2   cups coarsely chopped pecans or peanuts
1   cup flaked coconut
½   cup wheat germ
¾   cup firmly packed brown sugar
1   teaspoon ground cinnamon
½   teaspoon salt
¾   cup water
¾   cup vegetable oil
¼   cup honey
¼   cup molasses
1   teaspoon vanilla extract

Combine first 4 ingredients in a large bowl. Combine brown sugar and remaining ingredients in a saucepan; cook over medium heat, stirring often, until sugar dissolves. Pour hot mixture over cereal mixture; stir until thoroughly blended. (Mixture will appear wet.) Spread evenly in a lightly greased, large, shallow pan. Bake at 300° for 1 hour, stirring every 15 minutes. Cool; store in an airtight container.
Yield: 9½ cups.

Breads

PROGRESSIVE FARMER
JANUARY 1942

BASIC BUTTERMILK BISCUITS

Sift 2 cups whole wheat flour. Measure and add ¼ teaspoon soda and 1 teaspoon baking powder. Sift together; add 2 to 4 tablespoons fat and cut into flour mixture thoroughly.

Gradually add ¾ cup fresh buttermilk. Mix into soft dough.

Turn on a floured cloth or board (½ cup extra flour is used on the board for handling). Knead lightly, roll ½-inch thick, cut, and place on ungreased baking sheet.

Bake 12 to 15 minutes in a hot oven (450°). Yield: 18 average-sized family biscuits.

Banana-Oatmeal Bread

Vegetable cooking spray
1   teaspoon all-purpose flour
1½ cups all-purpose flour
¼   teaspoon salt
⅔   cup sugar
½   cup regular oats, uncooked
2¼ teaspoons baking powder
½   cup egg substitute
⅓   cup vegetable oil
1   cup mashed ripe bananas

Coat an 8½- x 4½- x 3-inch loafpan with cooking spray; dust with 1 teaspoon flour. Set aside.

Combine 1½ cups flour and next 4 ingredients in a large bowl; make a well in center of mixture.

Combine egg substitute, oil, and bananas; add to dry ingredients, stirring just until moistened. Spoon into prepared pan.

Bake at 350° for 55 minutes or until a wooden pick inserted in center comes out clean.

Cool in pan on a wire rack 10 minutes; remove from pan. Yield: 1 loaf.

Note: This is a low-fat recipe that has 138 calories per ½-inch slice, with 2.5g protein, 4.6g fat, 21.9g carbohydrate, 0.8g fiber, 0mg cholesterol, 85mg sodium, and 32mg calcium.

"There is no love sincerer than the love of food."

GEORGE BERNARD SHAW

Sweet Cinnamon Bread

2   cups all-purpose flour
1   tablespoon baking powder
1   teaspoon salt
1½ teaspoons ground cinnamon
1   cup sugar
2   large eggs, lightly beaten
1   cup buttermilk
⅓ cup vegetable oil
2   teaspoons vanilla extract
2   tablespoons sugar
1   teaspoon ground cinnamon
2   teaspoons butter or margarine, softened

Combine first 5 ingredients in a mixing bowl. Combine eggs and next 3 ingredients; add to dry ingredients. Beat at medium speed with an electric mixer 3 minutes.

Grease bottom of a 9- x 5- x 3-inch loafpan. Spoon half of batter into pan.

Combine 2 tablespoons sugar, 1 teaspoon cinnamon, and butter in a small bowl until crumbly. Spoon evenly over batter and top with remaining batter. Gently swirl batter with a knife to create a marbled effect.

Bake at 350° for 50 minutes or until a wooden pick inserted in center comes out clean.

Remove from pan immediately and cool completely on a wire rack. Yield: 1 loaf.

SARAH FOX, Corsicana, Tex.

Festive Cranberry Bread

⅓ cup butter or margarine, softened
1¼ cups sugar
2   large eggs
3   cups all-purpose flour
1   tablespoon baking powder
½   teaspoon salt
¾   cup water
⅓   cup orange juice
1½ cups fresh cranberries, coarsely chopped
½   cup chopped walnuts
1   tablespoon grated orange rind

Beat butter at medium speed with an electric mixer until creamy; gradually add sugar, beating well. Add eggs, one at a time, beating well. Combine flour, baking powder, and salt; add to butter mixture alternately with water and orange juice, beginning and ending with flour mixture. Mix after each addition. Stir in cranberries, walnuts, and orange rind.

Spoon batter into a greased and floured 9- x 5- x 3-inch loafpan.

Bake at 350° for 1 hour and 10 minutes or until a wooden pick inserted in center comes out clean. Cool in pan on a wire rack 10 minutes; remove from pan and let cool completely on wire rack. Yield: 1 loaf.

MRS. PARKE LAGOURGUE CORY, Neosho, Mo.

Jalapeño Cornbread

2½ cups yellow cornmeal
1   cup all-purpose flour
1   tablespoon plus 1 teaspoon baking powder
1   tablespoon salt
2   tablespoons sugar
½   cup nonfat dry milk
3   large eggs, lightly beaten
1½ cups water
½   cup vegetable oil
1   (17-ounce) can cream-style corn
3 to 4 jalapeño peppers, seeded and chopped
2   cups shredded sharp Cheddar cheese
1   cup minced onion

Combine first 6 ingredients; make a well in center of mixture.

Combine eggs, water, and oil; add to dry ingredients, stirring until moistened. Fold in corn and remaining ingredients. Spoon mixture into a greased 13- x 9- x 2-inch pan.

Bake at 425° for 35 minutes or until a knife inserted in center comes out clean. Yield: 15 servings.

"How can you govern a country which has 246 varieties of cheese?"

CHARLES DE GAULLE

Cheese-and-Pepper Muffins

3   tablespoons finely chopped green bell pepper
¼   cup finely chopped onion
1   (2-ounce) jar diced pimiento, drained
¾   cup (3 ounces) shredded sharp Cheddar cheese
2½ cups all-purpose flour
¼   cup yellow cornmeal
2   tablespoons baking powder
1   teaspoon salt
¼   teaspoon ground red pepper
¼   cup sugar
2   large eggs, lightly beaten
1½ cups milk
¼   cup shortening, melted

Combine first 10 ingredients in a medium bowl; make a well in center of mixture.

Combine eggs, milk, and shortening; add to dry ingredients, stirring just until moistened. Spoon into greased muffin pans, filling two-thirds full.

Bake at 400° for 20 to 25 minutes. Yield: 1½ dozen.

JEANNINE ALLEN, McAllen, Tex.

Fresh Apple Muffins

2   cups all-purpose flour
½   cup sugar
1   tablespoon baking powder
½   teaspoon salt
½   teaspoon ground cinnamon
½   teaspoon ground nutmeg
1½ cups peeled, chopped cooking apple, divided
1   cup milk
¼   cup vegetable oil
1   large egg, lightly beaten
¼   cup sugar
½   teaspoon ground cinnamon

Combine first 6 ingredients in a large bowl; stir in 1 cup apples and make a well in center of mixture.

Combine milk, oil, and egg; add to dry ingredients, stirring just until moistened. Spoon into greased muffin pans, filling two-thirds full.

Combine remaining ½ cup apple, ¼ cup sugar, and ½ teaspoon cinnamon; sprinkle over muffin batter. Bake at 350° for 20 to 25 minutes. Yield: 1 dozen.

MARIE JEFFERSON, Danville, Va.

"All happiness depends on a leisurely breakfast."

JOHN GUNTER

Sourdough Biscuits

2   cups biscuit mix
¾   cup plus 2 tablespoons Sourdough Starter

Combine biscuit mix and Sourdough Starter, stirring until biscuit mix is moistened.

Turn dough out onto a lightly floured surface and knead lightly 3 or 4 times.

Roll dough to ½-inch thickness; cut with a 2-inch biscuit cutter. Place on a lightly greased baking sheet with sides touching. Bake at 400° for 12 to 14 minutes. Yield: 16 biscuits.

Sourdough Starter

2   cups all-purpose flour
2   tablespoons sugar
1   package active dry yeast
2½ cups warm water (120° to 130°)

Combine first 3 ingredients in a medium-size non-metal bowl; gradually add warm water, mixing well. Cover loosely with plastic wrap; let stand in a warm place (85°) for 72 hours, stirring 1 or 2 times daily. Yield: 3 cups.

Note: For campfire cooking, place biscuits in an oiled 16-inch cast-iron Dutch oven. Cover and put away from fire. Place a few white-hot coals on lid. Allow biscuits to rise 10 to 15 minutes. Put more coals on lid; bake about 20 minutes.

Arrange coals on ground; set Dutch oven over coals. Spread additional coals evenly around bottom of the Dutch oven, placing 1 inch away. Continue to bake biscuits, replacing coals as needed. Check every 5 minutes until biscuits are done.

Quick Spoon Rolls

4 cups self-rising flour
1 cup instant nonfat dry milk powder
½ cup sugar
1 package active dry yeast
2 cups water
1 cup butter-flavored shortening
2 large eggs, lightly beaten

Combine first 4 ingredients in a large bowl; set aside.

Combine water and shortening in a saucepan; heat until shortening melts, stirring occasionally. Cool to 120° to 130°.

Add shortening mixture and eggs to flour mixture; stir until blended. Cover with heavy-duty plastic wrap; let stand 30 minutes. Spoon into lightly greased muffin pans.

Bake at 350° for 20 minutes or until golden brown. Remove from pans immediately. Yield: 2 dozen.

ESTELLE BRYANT, Greenwood, Miss.

"I never see any home cooking. All I get is fancy stuff."

PRINCE PHILIP, DUKE OF EDINBURGH

Herbed Dinner Rolls

4   cups all-purpose flour, divided
2   tablespoons sugar
2   packages active dry yeast
1   teaspoon dried basil
1   tablespoon fresh chives
1   teaspoon salt
1   teaspoon garlic salt
⅛   teaspoon dried rosemary
1   cup milk
½   cup water
2   tablespoons butter or margarine
1   large egg, lightly beaten
¼   cup butter or margarine, melted

Combine 2 cups flour, sugar, and next 6 ingredients in a large mixing bowl. Combine milk, water, and butter in a saucepan; heat until butter melts, stirring occasionally. Remove from heat and cool to 120° to 130°.

Gradually add liquid mixture to flour mixture, beating well at medium speed with an electric mixer until smooth. Add egg, beating well. Beat an additional 2 minutes at medium speed. Gradually add ¾ cup flour, beating 2 minutes at medium speed. Gradually stir in enough remaining flour to make a soft dough.

Turn dough out onto a floured surface and knead until smooth and elastic (about 10 minutes). Place in a well-greased bowl, turning to grease top. Cover and let rise in a warm place (85°), free from drafts, 45 minutes or until doubled in bulk.

Punch dough down; turn out onto a lightly floured surface and knead lightly 4 or 5 times. Divide dough into 16 portions; shape each portion into a ball. Dip balls into melted butter. Place in a greased 13- x 9- x 2-inch baking pan.

Let rolls rise in a warm place, free from drafts, for 15 to 20 minutes or until doubled in bulk. Bake at 375° for 20 minutes or until golden brown. Yield: 16 rolls.

Desserts

VINTAGE RECIPES

PROGRESSIVE FARMER
MAY 1914

STRAWBERRY WHIP

Put 1¼ cups strawberries, 1 cup powdered sugar, and the white of 1 egg in bowl and beat with wire whisk until stiff enough to hold shape. About 20 minutes will be required for beating. Pile lightly on dish; chill. Surround with lady fingers and serve with boiled custard.

PROGRESSIVE FARMER
JUNE 1908

BAKED PEACHES

Rub peaches with a coarse cloth to remove the down but do not cut. Stick 2 or 3 cloves in each and place side by side in a baking pan; sprinkle with sugar and add a very little water. Bake in a good heat until well cooked; serve hot or cold.

Italian Cream Cake

½ cup butter or margarine, softened
½ cup shortening
2 cups sugar
5 large eggs
2 cups all-purpose flour
1 teaspoon baking soda
1 cup buttermilk
1 teaspoon vanilla extract
1 (3½-ounce) can flaked coconut
1 cup chopped pecans
Italian Cream Frosting
½ cup finely chopped pecans

Beat butter and shortening at medium speed with an electric mixer until creamy. Gradually add sugar, beating well. Add eggs, one at a time, beating after each addition.

Combine flour and soda; add to creamed mixture alternately with buttermilk, beginning and ending with flour mixture. Mix after each addition. Stir in vanilla, coconut, and 1 cup pecans.

Spoon batter into 3 greased and floured 9-inch round cakepans. Bake at 350° for 20 to 23 minutes or until a wooden pick inserted in center comes out clean. Cool in pans on wire racks 10 minutes; remove from pans and let cool on wire racks.

Spread Italian Cream Frosting between layers and on top and sides of cake, sprinkling ½ cup pecans between layers and on top. Store in refrigerator.

Yield: one 3-layer cake.

Italian Cream Frosting

¼ cup butter or margarine, softened
1 (8-ounce) package cream cheese, softened
1 (16-ounce) package powdered sugar, sifted
1 teaspoon vanilla extract

Beat butter and cream cheese at medium speed with an electric mixer; gradually add powdered sugar, beating at low speed until of spreading consistency. Stir in vanilla. Yield: enough for one 3-layer cake.

GLENNETTA HOUCK, Cape Girardeau, Mo.

Caramel-Nut Pound Cake

1 **cup butter or margarine, softened**
½ **cup shortening**
2 **cups firmly packed brown sugar**
1 **cup sugar**
5 **large eggs**
3 **cups all-purpose flour**
½ **teaspoon baking powder**
½ **teaspoon salt**
1 **cup milk**
1 **tablespoon vanilla extract**
1 **cup finely chopped pecans**
Powdered sugar

Beat butter and shortening at medium speed with an electric mixer until creamy; gradually add sugars, beating well. Add eggs, one at a time, beating after each addition.

Combine flour, baking powder, and salt; add to creamed mixture alternately with milk, beginning and ending with flour mixture. Stir in vanilla and pecans.

Pour batter into a greased and floured 10-inch tube pan. Bake at 325° for 1½ hours or until a wooden pick inserted in center comes out clean. Cool in pan on a wire rack 10 minutes; remove from pan and cool completely on a wire rack. Sprinkle with powdered sugar. Yield: one 10-inch cake.

SELMA L. GRAHAM, Alvin, Tex.

Captivating Chocolate Torte

3 (1-ounce) squares unsweetened chocolate
½ cup butter or margarine, softened
2 cups firmly packed brown sugar
3 large eggs
1½ teaspoons vanilla extract
2 cups sifted cake flour
2 teaspoons baking soda
¼ teaspoon salt
¾ cup sour cream
2 teaspoons instant coffee granules
1 cup boiling water
½ cup strawberry preserves
Chocolate Frosting

Melt chocolate in top of a double boiler; set aside. Beat butter at medium speed with an electric mixer until creamy; gradually add brown sugar, beating well. Add eggs, one at a time, beating after each addition. Add chocolate and vanilla; beat until blended.

Combine flour, soda, and salt; add to butter mixture alternately with sour cream, beginning and ending with flour mixture. Beat after each addition.

Dissolve coffee granules in boiling water; stir into batter. Pour batter into 3 greased and floured 8-inch round cakepans. Bake at 350° for 25 to 30 minutes or until a wooden pick inserted in center comes out clean. Cool in pans on wire rack 10 minutes; remove from pans and let cool completely on wire rack.

Spread ¼ cup preserves between each layer. Frost top and sides of cake with Chocolate Frosting.

Yield: 1 (8-inch) torte.

Chocolate Frosting

8 (1-ounce) squares sweet baking chocolate
¼ cup water
¼ cup plus 2 tablespoons butter or margarine

Combine chocolate and water in a heavy saucepan; cook over low heat until chocolate melts, stirring often. Remove from heat; stir in butter. Let cool to spreading consistency, stirring occasionally. Yield: enough for 1 (8-inch) torte.

GLENDA MARIE STOKES, Florence, S.C.

Chocolate Ripple Pound Cake

3   **tablespoons shortening**
½   **cup plus 1 tablespoon cocoa**
2   **cups butter or margarine, softened**
3   **cups sugar**
10 **large eggs**
4   **cups sifted cake flour**
2   **teaspoons vanilla extract**

Melt shortening in a small saucepan; add cocoa, stirring until smooth. Set aside.

Beat butter at medium speed with an electric mixer until creamy; gradually add sugar, beating well. Add eggs, one at a time, beating after each addition. Add flour and vanilla, mixing well.

Remove 2 cups of batter and add chocolate mixture, stirring until blended. Spoon ⅓ remaining batter into a greased and floured 10-inch tube pan; top with half of chocolate batter. Repeat layers, ending with plain batter. Draw a knife through batter to make a swirl design. Bake at 325° for 1 hour and 30 minutes or until a wooden pick inserted in center comes out clean. Cool cake in pan on a wire rack 10 minutes; remove from pan and cool completely on a wire rack.

Yield: one 10-inch cake.

FRANCES B. GREENE, Troy, Ala.

Oatmeal Cake

1   cup quick-cooking oats, uncooked
1⅓ cups boiling water
½   cup butter or margarine, softened
½   cup firmly packed brown sugar
½   cup sugar
2   large eggs, lightly beaten
1   teaspoon vanilla extract
1⅓ cups all-purpose flour
1   teaspoon baking soda
½   teaspoon salt
1   teaspoon ground cinnamon
Topping

Combine oats and boiling water; let stand 20 minutes. Beat butter at medium speed with an electric mixer until creamy; gradually add sugars, beating well. Add eggs, vanilla, and oatmeal mixture, beating until blended. Combine flour and next 3 ingredients; add to butter mixture and stir until blended. Pour into a greased and floured 9-inch square baking dish. Bake at 325° for 35 minutes. Spread topping on hot cake; broil 5½ inches from heat (with electric oven door partially opened) 4 minutes. Cool. Yield: 9 servings.

Topping

½   cup evaporated milk
¼   cup firmly packed brown sugar
¼   cup sugar
¼   cup butter or margarine
1   cup flaked coconut
½   cup chopped pecans

Combine all ingredients in a medium saucepan; bring to a boil, stirring constantly. Yield: enough topping for one 9-inch cake.

MRS. REGIE HARTZOG, Ariton, Ala.

Cherry-Topped Cheesecake

2 cups graham cracker crumbs
½ cup butter or margarine, melted
¼ cup chopped pecans
3 (8-ounce) packages cream cheese, softened
1½ cups sugar
5 large eggs
3 tablespoons lemon juice
1 (24-ounce) can cherry pie filling

Combine graham cracker crumbs, butter, and pecans; press firmly into a 13- x 9- x 2-inch baking pan. Set aside.

Beat cream cheese at medium speed with an electric mixer until soft and creamy; gradually add sugar, beating until fluffy. Add eggs one at a time, beating after each addition. Stir in lemon juice.

Pour into prepared crust; bake at 350° for 45 minutes or until set. Cool on a wire rack. Spread pie filling on top; chill thoroughly. Yield: 15 to 18 servings.

MRS. NELSON SCHROCK, Kennedyville, Md.

> *"No diet will remove all the fat from your body because the brain is entirely fat. Without a brain you might look good, but all you could do is run for public office."*
>
> *COVERT BAILEY*

Berry Devonshire Tart

1   cup all-purpose flour
2   tablespoons sugar
¼   teaspoon salt
⅓   cup butter or margarine
1   egg yolk, lightly beaten
2   tablespoons cold water
2   (3-ounce) packages cream cheese, softened
2   tablespoons sugar
⅓   cup sour cream
1   quart fresh strawberries
1½ cups fresh raspberries
⅓   cup sugar
1   tablespoon cornstarch

Combine first 3 ingredients; cut in butter with pastry blender until mixture is crumbly. Combine egg yolk and water; sprinkle evenly over surface. Stir with a fork until dry ingredients are moistened.

Press dough onto bottom and sides of a lightly greased 9-inch tart pan. Prick bottom and sides of pastry with a fork. Bake at 400° for 15 minutes or until lightly browned. Cool; set aside.

Beat cream cheese and 2 tablespoons sugar in a small mixing bowl at high speed with an electric mixer until smooth. Stir in sour cream; spread evenly over cooled tart shell. Wash, dry, and hull strawberries. Arrange strawberries, stem side down, over cheese mixture. Chill.

Puree raspberries in blender. Strain puree and discard seed. Add enough water to puree to measure 1 cup. Combine ⅓ cup sugar and cornstarch in a small saucepan. Gradually add raspberry puree; cook over medium heat, stirring constantly, until mixture comes to a boil. Boil 1 minute. Pour over strawberries. Chill 2 to 3 hours. Yield: one 9-inch tart.

CHARLOTTE MALLET-PREVOST, Dickerson, Md.

Fruit Pizza

1   (20-ounce) package refrigerated sliceable sugar
      cookie dough
1   (8-ounce) package cream cheese, softened
⅓   cup sugar
½   teaspoon vanilla extract
1   cup fresh strawberries, halved
2   small bananas, sliced
1   medium peach, peeled and thinly sliced
½   cup halved seedless green grapes
½   medium apple, thinly sliced
¼   cup fresh blueberries
3   cantaloupe balls
½   cup orange marmalade
2   tablespoons water

Line a 12-inch pizza pan with foil, allowing foil to
overlap rim of pan. Cut cookie dough into ⅛-inch
slices. Arrange slices in circular pattern in pizza pan,
starting at outer edge of pan and overlapping slices at
center. Bake at 325° for 20 to 25 minutes or until lightly browned. Cool completely.

Combine cream cheese, sugar, and vanilla; beat
until smooth. Spread mixture over cooled cookie
crust. Arrange fruit over top as desired.

Combine marmalade and water; spoon evenly over
fruit. Chill. Before serving, transfer pizza to serving
platter. Yield: 6 to 8 servings.

RACHELLE CHANDLER, Parchman, Miss.

Blueberry Syrup

4 cups blueberries, crushed
1 cup water
½ cup sugar

Combine blueberries and water in a Dutch oven. Bring to a boil over medium heat; cover, reduce heat, and simmer 15 minutes.

Remove from heat and pour mixture through a wire-mesh strainer into a 2-cup liquid measure to remove 1⅓ cups juice, discarding pulp.

Combine juice and sugar in a medium saucepan; bring to a rolling boil over medium heat. Remove from heat. Let cool. Refrigerate until ready to serve.

Serve over pancakes, pound cake, or ice cream. Yield: 1¾ cups.

NELL O. LUFFMAN, Anthony, Fla.

Apple Crisp

¾ cup sugar
½ cup all-purpose flour
½ cup butter or margarine
8 cooking apples, peeled, cored, and thinly sliced
½ cup water
1 teaspoon ground cinnamon

Combine sugar and flour; cut in butter with a pastry blender until mixture is crumbly.

Place apples in a lightly greased 8-inch-square baking dish. Combine water and cinnamon; pour over apples.

Top with sugar mixture and bake, uncovered, at 400° for 50 minutes. Yield: 9 servings.

GAYNELL S. BURT, Fort Payne, Ala.

Baked Peach Halves

3   tablespoons dark brown sugar
¾   teaspoon ground ginger
¾   teaspoon grated lemon rind
2   (16-ounce) cans peach halves, drained

Combine first 3 ingredients; sprinkle evenly over top of each peach half. Bake at 375° for 8 to 10 minutes or until thoroughly heated. Serve hot.
Yield: 6 servings.

MRS. BRUCE FOWLER, Woodruff, S.C.

Blackberry-Apple Pie

3   cups peeled and thinly sliced apples
2   cups fresh or frozen blackberries, thawed and
       drained
2   tablespoons cranberry juice
2   tablespoons butter or margarine, melted
¾   cup sugar
2   tablespoons cornstarch
Pastry for double-crust 9-inch pie

Combine first 4 ingredients in a large bowl. Combine sugar and cornstarch; add to fruit mixture, tossing lightly. Set aside.
Roll half of pastry to ⅛-inch thickness and fit into a 9-inch pieplate. Spoon fruit into pastry. Roll remaining pastry to ⅛-inch thickness; transfer to top of pie. Trim pastry; seal and flute edges. Cut slits in top for steam to escape. Bake at 350° for 1 hour.
Yield: one 9-inch pie.

LUCY M. DUNCAN, Willis, Va.

Sweet Potato Pie

1½ cups cooked, mashed sweet potatoes
¾ cup sugar
1   cup milk
2   large eggs, lightly beaten
1   tablespoon all-purpose flour
2   teaspoons ground cinnamon
2   tablespoons butter or margarine
1   unbaked 9-inch pastry shell

Combine first 7 ingredients in a saucepan; cook over medium heat until butter melts, stirring constantly. Pour mixture into prepared pastry shell. Bake at 400° for 10 minutes; reduce heat to 350° and bake an additional 45 minutes or until set.
Yield: one 9-inch pie.

JAN RAMSEY, Quitaque, Tex.

Quick Coconut Pie

4   large eggs
2   cups milk
1½ cups sugar
½ cup all-purpose flour
¼ cup butter or margarine, melted
1   teaspoon vanilla extract
1   (7-ounce) can flaked coconut

Combine first 6 ingredients in container of an electric blender; process on low speed 3 minutes. Pour mixture into 2 lightly greased 8-inch pieplates and let stand 5 minutes. Sprinkle with coconut, pressing down into mixture. Bake at 350° for 35 to 40 minutes or until set. Chill before serving.
Yield: two 8-inch pies.

ROSE KUEHNLE, Brenham, Tex.

Fudge-Nut Pie

¼ cup butter or margarine
2 (1-ounce) squares unsweetened chocolate
3 large eggs, lightly beaten
¾ cup firmly packed brown sugar
1 cup light corn syrup
1 teaspoon vanilla extract
⅛ teaspoon salt
1 cup chopped pecans
1 unbaked 9-inch pastry shell
Pecan halves
Whipped cream (optional)

Combine butter and chocolate in a small saucepan; heat until melted. Set aside; cool.

Combine eggs and sugar; stir in chocolate mixture, corn syrup, vanilla, and salt. Stir in pecans. Pour into pastry shell. Bake at 350° for 45 minutes. Cool. Garnish with pecan halves. To serve, top each slice with whipped cream, if desired. Yield: one 9-inch pie.

SALLIE BACON, Stamps, Ark.

Honey Pecan Pie

1 cup honey
¼ cup butter or margarine, melted
3 large eggs, lightly beaten
1 teaspoon vanilla extract
⅛ teaspoon salt
1½ cups chopped pecans
1 unbaked 9-inch pastry shell

Combine first 5 ingredients; stir in pecans. Pour into unbaked pastry shell. Bake at 350° for 30 to 40 minutes. Yield: one 9-inch pie.

Peach Cobbler

1 cup all-purpose flour
1 cup sugar
2 teaspoons baking powder
1 cup milk
⅓ cup butter or margarine
3 tablespoons sugar
1½ teaspoons ground cinnamon
1 (29-ounce) can sliced peaches, undrained

Combine first 3 ingredients; stir in milk. Pour mixture into a lightly greased, shallow 2-quart casserole. Dot with butter. Combine 3 tablespoons sugar, cinnamon, and peaches.

Spoon peach mixture over batter; do not stir. Bake at 350° for 50 to 60 minutes or until browned.

Yield: 6 to 8 servings.

Apple Cobbler: Prepare cobbler, substituting 1 (20-ounce) can sliced apples, ¼ cup applesauce, and ¼ cup crushed pineapple for sliced peaches.

"The secret of good cooking is first, having a love of it .... If you're convinced cooking is drudgery, you're never going to be any good at it, and you might as well warm up something frozen."

JAMES BEARD

Huckleberry Cobbler

2   cups sugar
2   cups water
3   cups fresh or frozen huckleberries or blueberries,
        thawed and drained
3   tablespoons lemon juice
3   tablespoons cornstarch
¼   cup water
1   (11-ounce) package pie crust sticks
¼   cup cold water
2   tablespoons butter or margarine, melted

Combine sugar and 2 cups water in a large saucepan; bring to a boil. Reduce heat and cook 2 minutes, stirring occasionally. Add huckleberries and lemon juice.

Combine cornstarch and ¼ cup water, stirring until smooth; add to huckleberry mixture.

Bring to a boil; boil 1 minute, stirring constantly. Spoon half of huckleberry mixture into an 8-inch square baking dish. Set aside.

Crumble pie crust sticks into a bowl. Sprinkle ¼ cup cold water (1 tablespoon at a time) evenly over surface. Stir with a fork until dry ingredients are moistened. Divide pastry in half; shape each portion into a ball.

Roll each portion to ⅛-inch thickness on a lightly floured surface; cut to an 8-inch square. Place on a baking sheet; bake at 450° for 8 minutes or until browned. Repeat procedure. Brush baked pastry with butter while warm.

Place one baked pastry over huckleberries. Top with remaining huckleberry mixture. Place remaining baked pastry over huckleberries. Yield: 6 to 8 servings.

REGINA WHITE, Columbia, Miss.

Molasses Sugar Cookies

½   cup butter or margarine, melted
1   cup sugar
¼   cup molasses
1   large egg
2   cups all-purpose flour
1   teaspoon baking soda
½   teaspoon salt
1   teaspoon ground cinnamon
½   teaspoon ground cloves
Sugar

Combine first 4 ingredients. Combine flour, soda, salt, and spices; add to molasses mixture, stirring until smooth.

Shape dough into 1-inch balls and dip one side in sugar. Place 2 inches apart, sugar side up, on ungreased cookie sheet.

Bake at 375° for 6 to 8 minutes. (Tops will crack.) Remove to wire racks to cool completely.

Yield: about 4 dozen.

DENNY KERNS, Brevard, N.C.

"A great step toward independence is a good-humored stomach."

SENECA

Sour Cream Drop Cookies

½   cup shortening
1½ cups sugar
2   large eggs
2¾ cups all-purpose flour
1   teaspoon baking soda
½   teaspoon salt
1   (8-ounce) carton sour cream
1   teaspoon vanilla extract
½   teaspoon lemon extract
5   cups sifted powdered sugar
⅓ to ½ cup milk
1¾ teaspoons lemon juice
¾   cup chopped pecans

Beat shortening at medium speed with an electric mixer; gradually add sugar, beating well. Add eggs, beating until blended. Combine flour, soda, and salt; add to shortening mixture alternately with sour cream, beginning and ending with flour mixture. Mix just until blended after each addition; stir in flavorings. Cover and chill at least 1 hour.

Drop dough by heaping teaspoonfuls onto lightly greased cookie sheets. Bake at 400° for 6 to 8 minutes or just until cookies begin to brown around edges. Remove to wire racks to cool completely.

Combine powdered sugar, milk, and lemon juice. Spread a thin layer on each cookie; sprinkle with pecans. Yield: 8½ dozen.

LUCILLE DUNCAN, Willis, Va.

Gumdrop Cookies

1 cup shortening
1 cup sugar
1 cup firmly packed brown sugar
2 large eggs
1 teaspoon vanilla extract
2 cups all-purpose flour
1 teaspoon baking powder
1 teaspoon baking soda
2 cups regular oats, uncooked
1 cup flaked coconut
1 (13-ounce) package small gumdrops, halved

Cream shortening in a large mixing bowl; gradually add sugars, beating well at medium speed with an electric mixer.

Add eggs, one at a time, beating after each addition. Stir in vanilla.

Combine flour, baking powder, and soda. Gradually add to creamed mixture, mixing well. Stir in oats and coconut. Drop dough by teaspoonfuls 2 inches apart onto greased cookie sheets.

Arrange 2 or 3 gumdrop halves on top of each cookie. Bake at 350° for 10 to 12 minutes or until lightly browned. Remove from cookie sheets immediately and cool on wire racks. Yield: 7½ dozen.

Christmas Jewels

4   (8-ounce) packages whole pitted dates, chopped
1¾ cups chopped Brazil nuts
1⅔ cups chopped walnuts
1½ cups chopped almonds
1   cup chopped candied cherries
1   cup chopped candied pineapple
½   cup all-purpose flour
1   cup butter or margarine, softened
1½ cups firmly packed brown sugar
3   large eggs
2½ cups all-purpose flour
1   teaspoon baking soda
1   teaspoon salt
1   teaspoon ground cinnamon
1½ teaspoons vanilla extract
Candied cherry halves (optional)

Combine first 6 ingredients; sprinkle with ½ cup flour, tossing to coat. Set aside.

Beat butter at medium speed with an electric mixer; gradually add sugar, beating well. Add eggs, one at a time, beating after each addition.

Combine 2½ cups flour and next 3 ingredients; add to butter mixture, mixing well. Stir in vanilla. Fold in fruit mixture. Drop dough by rounded teaspoonfuls onto lightly greased cookie sheets. Top with candied cherry halves, if desired.

Bake at 350° for 10 to 12 minutes or until browned. Remove to wire rack to cool completely. Yield: 14½ dozen.

MILDRED GOERING, Pretty Prairie, Kans.

Chewy Chocolate Cookies

½ cup shortening
1 cup sugar
1 large egg
1 teaspoon vanilla extract
1¾ cups all-purpose flour
½ teaspoon baking soda
¼ teaspoon salt
½ cup cocoa
½ cup milk
½ cup chopped pecans
24 large marshmallows, cut in half
Chocolate Frosting
Pecan halves

Beat shortening at medium speed with an electric mixer; gradually add sugar, beating well.

Add egg and vanilla; beat well.

Combine flour, soda, salt, and cocoa; gradually add to shortening mixture alternately with milk, beginning and ending with flour mixture. Mix well after each addition. Stir in chopped pecans.

Drop dough by rounded teaspoonfuls onto lightly greased cookie sheets. Bake at 350° for 8 minutes. Remove from oven; place a marshmallow half, cut side down, on top of each cookie. Return to oven; bake 2 additional minutes. Remove to wire racks to cool completely. Spread Chocolate Frosting on top and sides of marshmallows; top with a pecan half. Yield: 4 dozen.

Chocolate Frosting

2 cups sifted powdered sugar
¼ cup plus 1 tablespoon cocoa
3 tablespoons butter or margarine, softened
¼ cup milk

Combine all ingredients; beat at medium speed with an electric mixer until light and fluffy. Yield: 1 cup.

Pumpkin Pudding

3   large eggs, lightly beaten
1   (16-ounce) can pumpkin
1   (12-ounce) can evaporated milk
½   cup butter or margarine, melted
1   teaspoon vanilla extract
1   cup sugar
½   cup self-rising flour
½   teaspoon ground cinnamon
½   teaspoon ground nutmeg
Whipped cream (optional)

Combine first 5 ingredients in a large bowl. Combine sugar and next 3 ingredients; add to pumpkin mixture, stirring until well blended. Pour into a lightly greased 11- x 7- x 1½-inch baking dish. Bake at 400° for 25 minutes or until set. Serve with whipped cream, if desired. Yield: 8 to 10 servings.

ANNA MAY JOINES, Hickory, N.C.

Biscuit Pudding

2   large eggs, lightly beaten
2   cups milk
1   cup sugar
½   teaspoon vanilla extract
1   teaspoon ground cinnamon
¼   teaspoon ground nutmeg
3   cups crumbled biscuits

Combine first 6 ingredients; stir in biscuits. Spoon into a lightly greased 2-quart casserole. Bake at 350° for 20 to 25 minutes or until a knife inserted in center comes out clean. Yield: 6 servings.

MRS. W. T. WELCH, San Angelo, Tex.

Old-Fashioned Cracker Pudding

3   large eggs, separated
¾   cup sugar
Pinch of salt
2   cups milk
1   cup crushed crackers
½   cup flaked coconut
1   teaspoon vanilla extract
Pinch of salt
¼   cup sugar
¼   teaspoon vanilla extract
3   tablespoons flaked coconut

Combine egg yolks and next 3 ingredients in a medium saucepan. Add crackers and ½ cup coconut; beat well.

Cook over medium heat, stirring constantly, until mixture thickens. Stir in 1 teaspoon vanilla. Spoon mixture into a 10- x 6- x 2-inch baking dish.

Beat egg whites (at room temperature) and a pinch of salt until foamy. Add ¼ cup sugar, 1 tablespoon at a time, beating until stiff peaks form. Add ¼ teaspoon vanilla and beat until blended. Spread meringue over pudding, sealing to edge of dish; sprinkle with 3 tablespoons coconut. Bake at 325° for 25 minutes or until golden brown. Yield: 6 servings.

> *"The proof of the pudding is in the eating."*
>
> MIGUEL DE CERVANTES

Deluxe Peach Ice Cream

6   cups mashed peaches
1   cup sugar
3   large eggs
1½ cups sugar
2   tablespoons all-purpose flour
½ teaspoon salt
1   quart milk
1   cup whipping cream
1   tablespoon vanilla extract

Combine peaches and 1 cup sugar; set aside.

Beat eggs at medium speed with an electric mixer until frothy. Combine sugar, flour, and salt; gradually add to eggs, beating until thick. Add milk; mix well.

Pour egg mixture into a large saucepan. Cook over low heat, stirring constantly, until mixture thickens and coats a metal spoon (about 15 minutes). Remove from heat and set pan in cold water; stir gently until cool. Stir in whipping cream and vanilla. Add peaches, stirring well. Pour mixture into freezer can of a 1-gallon hand-turned or electric freezer. Freeze according to manufacturer's instructions. Pack freezer with additional ice and rock salt and let stand 1 hour before serving. Yield: about 1 gallon.

Chocolate Fudge Ice Cream

2   (14-ounce) cans sweetened condensed milk
2   (4-ounce) packages chocolate instant pudding mix
2   quarts milk

Combine all ingredients in a large bowl. Pour mixture into freezer can of a 5-quart hand-turned or electric freezer. Freeze according to manufacturer's instructions. Serve at once. Yield: about 1 gallon.

KENDA FAULKNER, Miami, Tex.

Extra-Special Chocolate Ice Cream

8   ounces milk chocolate, chopped
3   cups half-and-half
1   cup whipping cream
4   egg yolks, lightly beaten
¾   cup sugar
½   teaspoon ground cinnamon
1½ tablespoons vanilla extract
¼   teaspoon almond extract

Place chocolate in a small saucepan; cook over low heat until chocolate melts. Remove from heat.

Combine half-and-half and whipping cream in a 3-quart saucepan; cook over low heat until hot.

Combine egg yolks, sugar, and cinnamon. Gradually stir about one-fourth of hot mixture into egg mixture; add to remaining hot mixture, stirring constantly.

Cook over low heat 7 minutes or until slightly thickened, stirring constantly; remove from heat. Stir in melted chocolate and flavorings; cover and chill 3 hours, stirring occasionally.

Pour into freezer can of a 1-gallon hand-turned or electric freezer. Freeze according to manufacturer's instructions. Pack freezer with additional ice and rock salt and let stand 1 hour before serving.

Yield: about 2 quarts.

PAM MILLER, Clinton, Miss.

Main Dishes

VINTAGE RECIPES

PROGRESSIVE FARMER
JANUARY 1932

RABBIT PIE

Skin and dress a rabbit; soak for 1 hour in tepid water and cut into small pieces. Wipe dry, rub with lemon juice, salt, and pepper. Put into a quart of water; bring to boiling point and simmer until tender.

Make a rich pastry and line a deep pan. Put into a hot oven and bake until light brown. Then put the rabbit into the pan, cover with gravy made from the liquid where it was cooked, and dot with butter.

Cover with a top crust and bake in a hot oven (450°) for 25 to 35 minutes until done.

Beef Tenderloin Stuffed With Mushrooms

Vegetable cooking spray
1   pound fresh mushrooms, sliced
1   cup chopped green onions
¼   cup chopped fresh parsley
1   (5- to 6-pound) beef tenderloin
½   teaspoon salt-free herb-and-spice blend
½   cup reduced-sodium soy sauce
⅓   cup dry sherry
2   tablespoons honey
2   tablespoons light brown sugar
1   tablespoon vegetable oil
2   cloves garlic, minced

Coat a large, nonstick skillet with cooking spray; place over medium-high heat until hot. Add mushrooms and green onions; cook until tender. Drain; stir in parsley. Set aside.

Trim excess fat from tenderloin. Cut tenderloin lengthwise from top to within ½ inch of bottom, leaving bottom connected. Sprinkle cut edges with herb blend. Spoon mushroom mixture into opening of tenderloin; pull sides together. Tie tenderloin securely with heavy string at 2-inch intervals. Place tenderloin in a large, shallow dish; set aside.

Combine soy sauce and remaining ingredients; pour over tenderloin. Cover and refrigerate 8 hours, basting occasionally with marinade.

Drain tenderloin and place on a rack in a roasting pan; insert meat thermometer, making sure it does not touch stuffing. Bake at 425° for 45 to 60 minutes or until meat thermometer registers 150° (medium) or until desired degree of doneness.

Transfer to serving platter; let stand 10 to 15 minutes before slicing. Yield: 11 servings.

Savory Pot Roast

1   (4- to 5-pound) boneless chuck roast
2   tablespoons vegetable oil
1   cup chopped onion
1½ cups water
1   (8-ounce) can tomato sauce
1   beef-flavored bouillon cube
1½ teaspoons salt
½   teaspoon fines herbes
⅛   teaspoon pepper
1   pound carrots, scraped and cut into thin strips
1   (32-ounce) jar sauerkraut, drained
2   tablespoons chopped parsley (optional)
1   tablespoon all-purpose flour
¼   cup water

Brown roast on both sides in hot oil in a large Dutch oven. Remove roast, reserving pan drippings. Cook onion in pan drippings until tender; stir in next 6 ingredients.

Bring mixture to a boil, stirring frequently. Add roast; cover, reduce heat, and simmer 2½ hours. Add carrots; cover and simmer 30 additional minutes.

Place sauerkraut in a saucepan; cook over medium heat until thoroughly heated, stirring occasionally.

Put roast and carrots on a platter, reserving pan drippings. Spoon sauerkraut around roast; sprinkle roast with parsley, if desired.

Combine flour and ¼ cup water, stirring until smooth; stir into pan drippings. Cook over medium heat, stirring constantly, until thickened and bubbly. Serve gravy with roast. Yield: 8 to 10 servings.

FLORA BOWIE, Splendora, Tex.

Basil Beef Roast

1 (3- to 3½-pound) boneless chuck roast
1 tablespoon vegetable oil
1 tablespoon dried basil, crushed
½ teaspoon garlic powder
½ teaspoon pepper
1 small onion, sliced and separated into rings
1 cup water

Brown roast on both sides in hot oil in a large Dutch oven. Sprinkle roast with basil, garlic powder, and pepper; top with onion. Add water.

Bring to a boil; cover, reduce heat, and simmer 2½ hours or until tender. Remove from pan drippings to serve. Yield: 6 to 8 servings.

MRS. O.D. ROGERS, Springville, Tenn.

Grilled Teriyaki Steaks

1¼ cups soy sauce
¼ cup vegetable oil
2 tablespoons white vinegar
¼ teaspoon ground ginger
1 clove garlic, minced
4 (1-inch-thick) beef tenderloin steaks (about 1¼ pounds)

Combine first 5 ingredients in an 8-inch square dish; add steaks, turning to coat. Cover and refrigerate 8 hours, turning steaks occasionally.

Remove steaks from marinade; discard marinade. Cook without grill lid over hot coals (400° to 500°) 16 to 20 minutes or to desired degree of doneness, turning once. Yield: 4 servings.

Barbecued Brisket

1   (5- to 6-pound) beef brisket
1   teaspoon salt
½   teaspoon pepper
1   teaspoon minced garlic
4   medium onions, thinly sliced
2   cups water, divided
2   (8-ounce) cans tomato sauce
½   cup chopped onion
¼   cup Worcestershire sauce
¼   cup butter or margarine, melted
2   tablespoons lemon juice
2   tablespoons white vinegar
2   teaspoons chili powder
1   teaspoon minced garlic
⅛   teaspoon hot sauce
3   tablespoons cornstarch

Trim excess fat from brisket and place fat side up in a roasting pan. Sprinkle with salt, pepper, and garlic. Place onion slices over meat.

Bake, uncovered, at 350° for 1½ hours. Combine 1½ cups water, tomato sauce, and next 8 ingredients; pour over brisket. Cover with aluminum foil and bake 2 hours or until tender, spooning sauce over brisket occasionally.

Transfer brisket to serving platter and pour pan juices into a saucepan.

Combine cornstarch and remaining ½ cup water. Gradually add to pan juices, stirring constantly. Bring to a boil; boil 1 minute, stirring constantly. Serve with brisket. Yield: 8 to 10 servings.

ROSE KUEHULE, Brenham, Tex.

Kansas Barbecued Steak

½   cup plus 1 tablespoon catsup
¼   cup firmly packed brown sugar
2   tablespoons butter or margarine
2¼ teaspoons lemon juice
1½ teaspoons liquid smoke
1½ teaspoons Worcestershire sauce
1   (2-to-3-pound) sirloin steak

Combine first 6 ingredients in a medium saucepan. Bring to a boil; reduce heat and simmer, uncovered, 30 minutes. Stir occasionally; set aside.

Cook steak, covered with grill lid, over medium coals (300° to 350°) until meat begins to brown; turn over and brush with sauce. Cook, covered, until other side begins to brown; turn and brush with sauce.

Grill 20 additional minutes or until desired degree of doneness, turning and basting occasionally with sauce. Serve with remaining sauce.

Yield: 4 servings.

> *" 'Bless thy good creatures to our use, and us to thy table' was the grace before meals at my school, and it seems to me to sum up admirably a truly balanced attitude to the pleasures of food and drink."*
>
> *BERNARD LEVIN*

Grillades and Grits

1½ pounds boneless top round steak, tenderized
¼   cup all-purpose flour
½   teaspoon salt
½   teaspoon pepper
⅓   cup bacon drippings, divided
1½ cups sliced onion
1   cup chopped red bell pepper
½   cup chopped celery
2   cloves garlic, minced
2   tablespoons all-purpose flour
1¼ cups beef broth
1½ cups chopped fresh tomatoes or canned
      tomatoes with juice
2   tablespoons Worcestershire sauce
½   teaspoon dried thyme
½   teaspoon hot sauce
Cooked grits

Trim excess fat from steak; pound steak to ¼-inch thickness, using a meat mallet. Cut into 2-inch squares. Combine flour, salt, and pepper; dredge steak in flour mixture.

Cook steak in 3 tablespoons bacon drippings in a large skillet until no longer pink, turning once; remove from skillet.

Add onion and next 3 ingredients; cook until crisp-tender. Push vegetable mixture to one side of skillet; add flour and remaining bacon drippings. Cook over medium heat, stirring constantly, until roux is the color of chocolate.

Add meat, beef broth, and next 4 ingredients; cover and simmer 1 to 1½ hours or until tender. Serve over grits. Yield: 6 servings.

Stuffed Cabbage Rolls

8   cups water
12   large cabbage leaves
1   pound ground beef
1   teaspoon salt
½   teaspoon pepper
½   teaspoon poultry seasoning
1   small onion, chopped
1   cup cooked rice
1   large egg
1   (15-ounce) can tomato sauce
¼   cup water
1   tablespoon brown sugar
1   tablespoon lemon juice

Bring water to a boil in a large Dutch oven. Add cabbage leaves; cover and remove from heat. Let stand 5 minutes; drain. Combine ground beef and next 6 ingredients.

Place equal portions of meat mixture in center of each cabbage leaf. Fold 2 opposite ends over and roll up. Secure with wooden picks.

Combine tomato sauce and remaining ingredients in a lightly greased, large skillet; stir well. Arrange cabbage rolls in skillet.

Cover and simmer over low heat 1 hour, basting frequently. Yield: 4 to 6 servings.

JULIE SWANSON, Akron, Iowa

Zucchini Lasagna

½ pound ground beef
½ cup chopped onion
1   (15-ounce) can tomato sauce
½ teaspoon salt
½ teaspoon dried oregano
¼ teaspoon dried basil
⅛ teaspoon pepper
4   medium zucchini (about 1¼ pounds), thinly sliced
        and divided
2   tablespoons all-purpose flour, divided
1   (12-ounce) container cottage cheese
1   large egg
1   cup (4 ounces) shredded mozzarella cheese

Cook beef and onion in a skillet until meat is browned, stirring until it crumbles; drain off pan drippings. Stir in tomato sauce and next 4 ingredients; bring to a boil. Reduce heat and simmer, uncovered, for 5 minutes, stirring occasionally.

Layer half of zucchini in a 11- x 7- x 1½-inch baking dish. Sprinkle with 1 tablespoon flour. Combine cottage cheese and egg; spread over zucchini. Spoon half of meat sauce over cottage cheese mixture, spreading evenly.

Repeat layers with zucchini, flour, and meat sauce. Bake at 375° for 35 minutes or until thoroughly heated. Sprinkle with mozzarella cheese and bake 5 additional minutes. Yield: 6 servings.

KAREN JEFFERSON, Chesapeake, Va.

Italian Baked Chicken

1   3- to 3½-pound) broiler-fryer, cut up and skinned
½   cup commercial Italian salad dressing
¼   teaspoon paprika

Dip chicken in salad dressing. Arrange in a lightly greased 13- x 9- x 2-inch baking dish. Sprinkle with paprika. Cover and bake at 350° for 45 minutes; uncover and bake 15 to 20 additional minutes.
Yield: 4 servings.

IRMA MARSHALL, Greenup, Ill.

Cola Chicken

1   (2½- to 3-pound) broiler-fryer, cut up and skinned
¼   cup butter or margarine, melted
1   green or red bell pepper, diced
1   large onion, diced
1   (10¾-ounce) can cream of mushroom soup, undiluted
1½ cups cola-flavored carbonated beverage
Hot cooked rice

Brown chicken in butter in a large skillet 5 minutes on each side or until golden. Remove from skillet, reserving drippings in skillet. Place chicken in an 11- x 7- x 1½-inch baking dish; set aside.
Cook pepper and onion in reserved drippings until crisp-tender; stir in soup and cola-flavored beverage. Pour over chicken; bake, uncovered, at 350° for 1 hour or until done.
Serve over rice. Yield: 4 servings.

CATHY PURVIS, Gadsden, Ala.

Chicken Tetrazzini

1   (3- to 3½-pound) broiler-fryer
2   quarts water
1   teaspoon salt
¼   cup plus 2 tablespoons butter or margarine
¼   cup plus 2 tablespoons all-purpose flour
2   cups milk
1   (10¾-ounce) can cream of mushroom soup,
       undiluted
1   cup chopped green bell pepper
1   (4-ounce) jar diced pimiento
1   (8-ounce) loaf process cheese spread, cut into
       cubes
¾   teaspoon garlic powder
½   teaspoon salt
1   (8-ounce) package egg noodles
½   cup soft breadcrumbs
1   tablespoon chopped fresh parsley

Place chicken in a Dutch oven; add water and salt.
Bring to a boil; cover, reduce heat, and simmer 45
minutes or until tender. Remove chicken and let cool,
reserving broth for other uses. Skin and bone chicken;
cut into bite-size pieces.

Melt butter in a heavy saucepan over low heat; add
flour, stirring until smooth. Cook 1 minute, stirring
constantly. Gradually add milk; cook over medium
heat, stirring constantly, until thickened and bubbly.
Add soup and next 5 ingredients, stirring until cheese
melts. Stir in chicken.

Cook noodles according to package directions;
drain. Arrange noodles in a lightly greased 13- x 9- x 2-
inch baking dish; spread chicken mixture over noodles. Sprinkle with breadcrumbs and parsley. Bake at
325° for 45 minutes. Yield: 6 to 8 servings.

MARIE M. MEYER, Kremlin, Okla.

Chilled Crispy Chicken

1⅓ cups cornflake crumbs
½ teaspoon salt
¼ teaspoon pepper
⅛ teaspoon paprika
1 (2½- to 3-pound) broiler-fryer, cut up
¼ teaspoon salt
¼ teaspoon pepper
⅛ teaspoon poultry seasoning
⅔ cup mayonnaise or salad dressing
4 lettuce leaves
8 tomato slices
12 cucumber slices
Mayonnaise or salad dressing

Combine first 4 ingredients in a plastic bag. Close bag and shake to blend ingredients; set aside.

Skin chicken, if desired. Sprinkle with ¼ teaspoon salt, ¼ teaspoon pepper, and poultry seasoning. Spread ⅔ cup mayonnaise evenly on both sides of chicken. Place 2 or 3 pieces at a time in bag of crumb mixture; shake well.

Place coated chicken in a lightly greased 13- x 9- x 2-inch baking dish.

Bake, uncovered, at 350° for 1 hour or until done. Let cool slightly. Cover and chill several hours. Serve chicken with lettuce, tomato, and cucumber slices; top with a dollop of mayonnaise. Yield: 4 servings.

KATIE HARMON, Elk Park, N.C.

Baked Orange Chicken

6   chicken breast halves, skinned
¼   cup butter or margarine, melted
2   tablespoons all-purpose flour
1½ cups orange juice
½   teaspoon salt
⅛   teaspoon ground cinnamon
1   orange, sliced

Brown chicken in butter in a large skillet; remove chicken. Add flour, stirring until smooth. Cook 1 minute, stirring constantly.

Gradually add orange juice; cook over medium heat, stirring constantly, until thickened and bubbly. Stir in salt and cinnamon. Remove from heat.

Arrange chicken in a lightly greased 13- x 9- x 2-inch baking dish and top with orange slices. Pour sauce over chicken. Bake, uncovered, at 350° for 1 hour, basting occasionally. Yield: 6 servings.

JUDY HUTCHENS, Waldron, Ark.

> *"I want every laborer in my realm to be able to put a fowl in the pot on Sunday."*
>
> *HENRI IV*

Chicken Piccata

⅓   cup all-purpose flour
1½ teaspoons salt
¼   teaspoon pepper
6   chicken breast halves, skinned and boned
¼   cup butter or margarine
¼   cup lemon juice
1   lemon, thinly sliced
2   tablespoons chopped fresh parsley
Garnishes: Fresh parsley sprigs, lemon wedges

Combine flour, salt, and pepper; dredge chicken in flour mixture. Set aside.

Melt butter in a large skillet over medium heat. Add chicken and cook 5 minutes on each side or until golden brown. Add lemon juice and slices; cover and cook 5 minutes or until chicken is done. Sprinkle with parsley. Garnish, if desired. Yield: 6 servings.

Pasta-Chicken Salad

1½ cups small shell macaroni, uncooked
4   cups diced, cooked chicken
1   cup mayonnaise
½   cup chopped sweet pickles
½   cup diced celery
1   small onion, chopped
1   teaspoon salt
½   teaspoon pepper
Lettuce leaves

Cook macaroni according to package directions, omitting salt; drain. Rinse with cold water; drain.

Combine pasta, chicken, and next 6 ingredients, tossing well; chill. Spoon into a lettuce-lined bowl. Yield: 8 servings.

MRS. META ZINSMEISTER, Boerne, Tex.

Glazed Chicken and Apples

²⁄₃ cup unsweetened apple juice
1 tablespoon white vinegar
2 teaspoons cornstarch
1 teaspoon chicken-flavored bouillon granules
¼ teaspoon ground cinnamon
Vegetable cooking spray
2 teaspoons vegetable oil
1 pound skinned, boned chicken breast halves,
   cut into ½-inch strips
¼ cup chopped onion
¼ cup shredded carrot
2 small apples, cored and cut into ¼-inch rings
Garnish: fresh parsley sprigs

Combine first 5 ingredients in a small bowl; set aside.

Coat a large, nonstick skillet with cooking spray and add oil; place over medium-high heat until hot. Add chicken; cook 2 minutes, stirring frequently. Add onion and carrot; cook 1 minute or until chicken is no longer pink.

Stir in apple juice mixture; cook, stirring constantly, until thickened. Add apple rings and toss gently. Cover, reduce heat, and simmer 3 minutes or until apples are tender. Garnish, if desired.

Yield: 4 servings.

Note: This receipe has 209 calories per 3 ounces of chicken and 4 apple rings with sauce, with 26.6g protein, 4.3g fat, 15.4g carbohydrate, 2.1g fiber, 66mg cholesterol, 283mg sodium, and 25mg calcium.

CAROL DOUIS, Davie, Fla.

Lemon-Garlic Turkey Breast

¼ cup freshly squeezed lemon juice
3 tablespoons chopped fresh parsley
1 tablespoon vegetable oil
3 cloves garlic, minced
1 teaspoon grated lemon rind
½ teaspoon paprika
½ teaspoon pepper
1 (6-pound) turkey breast, skinned and boned

Combine first 7 ingredients in a small bowl. Set aside.

Rinse turkey with water; pat dry. Brush cut side with half of lemon juice mixture. Loosely roll turkey breast and tie in several places with string.

Place in a large cooking bag prepared according to package directions. Pour remaining lemon juice mixture over turkey.

Seal bag; cut six ½-inch slits in top of bag to allow steam to escape. Insert meat thermometer. Place in a 13- x 9- x 2-inch baking dish.

Bake at 325° until meat thermometer registers 170° (about 1½ hours). Let stand 15 minutes; cut into thin slices. Yield: 18 servings.

Note: This receipe has 126 calories per 3-ounce serving, with 26.1g protein, 1.4g fat, 0.6g carbohydrate, 72mg cholesterol, 45mg sodium, and 13mg calcium.

Italian Turkey Cutlets

½ cup Italian-seasoned breadcrumbs
3 tablespoons all-purpose flour
3 tablespoons grated Parmesan cheese
¾ teaspoon dried oregano
⅛ teaspoon garlic powder
6 to 8 turkey cutlets (about 1½ pounds)
1 large egg, lightly beaten
⅓ cup vegetable oil
Garnishes: parsley sprigs, red bell pepper strips

Combine first 5 ingredients. Brush turkey cutlets on all sides with egg and dredge in breadcrumb mixture. Pour oil into a large, heavy skillet. Fry turkey in oil over medium heat 2 to 3 minutes on each side or until golden brown. Drain on paper towels. Garnish, if desired. Yield: 6 to 8 servings.

Turkey Salad

2 cups chopped cooked turkey
1 cup sliced celery
¼ cup chopped onion
½ cup mayonnaise
1 tablespoon chutney
1 teaspoon grated lemon rind
1 tablespoon lemon juice
1 teaspoon curry powder
½ teaspoon salt
Lettuce leaves
Garnishes: tomato wedges

Combine first 9 ingredients in a bowl. Cover and chill. To serve, spoon mixture onto lettuce leaves and garnish, if desired. Yield: 4 servings.

ANNA MAY JOINES, Hickory, N.C.

Baked Burgundy Ham

1   (6- to 8-pound) smoked fully cooked ham half
6   cups water
2   cups cranberry juice drink, divided
2   cups Burgundy, or other dry red wine, divided
2   cups firmly packed dark brown sugar, divided
2   (3-inch) sticks cinnamon
Whole cloves
1   cup raisins
**Garnishes: spiced crabapples, fresh parsley, fresh
    cranberries, raisins**

Trim skin from ham and discard; place ham in a large Dutch oven. Add water, 1 cup cranberry juice, 1 cup Burgundy, 1 cup brown sugar, and cinnamon sticks. Bring to a boil; cover, reduce heat, and simmer 20 minutes. Cool. Cover and refrigerate 8 hours, turning ham once.

Remove ham from marinade, reserving 2 cups marinade. Score fat on ham in a diamond design and stud with cloves. Place ham, fat side up, in a shallow roasting pan; insert meat thermometer, making sure it does not touch fat or bone.

Add raisins, 12 cloves, reserved marinade, remaining cranberry juice, Burgundy, and brown sugar to pan; stir. Cover and bake at 325° for 1½ hours. Uncover and bake an additional 15 minutes or until thermometer reaches 140°, basting ham occasionally with pan juices. Garnish, if desired.

Pour hot pan juices into a saucepan and bring to a boil; cook 20 minutes and serve with ham.

Yield: 12 to 14 servings.

Baked Ham Slices

1   cup water
¼   cup white vinegar
¼   cup catsup
3   tablespoons brown sugar
1   tablespoon Worcestershire sauce
4   (½- to ¾-inch-thick) smoked fully cooked
     ham slices

Combine first 5 ingredients in a 13- x 9- x 2-inch baking dish; place ham in dish and cover tightly. Refrigerate 2 to 4 hours. Remove from refrigerator and let stand 30 minutes. Bake, covered, at 350° for 30 to 40 minutes or until thoroughly heated, basting occasionally. Yield: 12 servings.

Ham-and-Potato Casserole

1   (10¾-ounce) can cream of mushroom soup,
     undiluted
1   cup milk
⅛   teaspoon pepper
3   cups thinly sliced peeled potatoes (2 large)
1½ to 2 cups chopped, cooked ham
1   small onion, chopped
½   cup (2 ounces) shredded Cheddar cheese
Paprika

Combine first 3 ingredients in a small saucepan; cook over medium heat until bubbly.

Layer potatoes, ham, onion, and cheese in a lightly greased 2-quart casserole. Pour soup mixture over cheese. Sprinkle with paprika. Cover and bake at 350° for 1 hour. Uncover and bake 15 additional minutes. Yield: 4 servings.

JANICE C. DISHMAN, Danville, Va.

Herbed Pork Chops

1   cup unsweetened pineapple juice
⅔   cup dry sherry
½   teaspoon dried rosemary leaves, crushed
4   (1-inch-thick) center-cut pork chops

Combine first 3 ingredients; set aside.

Arrange pork chops in an 8-inch square dish. Pour marinade over pork chops; cover and refrigerate 8 hours, turning meat occasionally.

Drain meat, discarding marinade. Place chops on a lightly greased rack in broiler pan. Broil 6 inches from heat (with electric oven door partially opened) 12 minutes. Turn chops and broil 10 additional minutes or until done. Yield: 4 servings.

FRANCES FENTON, Columbia, Mo.

Pork Chop Casserole

4   medium potatoes, peeled and sliced
1   small onion, chopped
½   teaspoon salt
Dash of pepper
1   (10¾-ounce) can cream of mushroom soup, undiluted
⅔   cup evaporated milk
4   (¾-inch-thick) pork chops

Alternate layers of potatoes, onion, salt, and pepper in a lightly greased 2-quart baking dish. Combine soup and milk; pour over potato mixture.

Trim fat from pork chops; brown both sides in a skillet. Place on top of potato mixture. Cover and bake at 350° for 1 hour and 20 minutes or until tender. Yield: 4 servings.

MARGARET DAUGHERTY, Jacksboro, Tenn.

Pork Stir-Fry

3   tablespoons vegetable oil, divided
2   tablespoons soy sauce, divided
3½ tablespoons cornstarch, divided
½ teaspoon garlic powder
¼ teaspoon pepper
1½ pounds boneless pork loin chops, cut into
     thin strips
4   carrots, scraped and thinly sliced
1   green bell pepper, cut into 1-inch pieces
8   green onions, cut into ½-inch slices
⅔   cup water
¾ teaspoon chicken-flavored bouillon granules
⅛ teaspoon ground ginger
Hot cooked rice

Combine 1 tablespoon oil, 1 tablespoon soy sauce, 1½ teaspoons cornstarch, garlic powder, and pepper. Add pork; stir and let stand 20 minutes.

Pour remaining 2 tablespoons oil around top of preheated wok or skillet, coating sides; heat at medium-high (325°) for 2 minutes. Add carrots and pepper; stir-fry 4 minutes. Add green onions; stir-fry 2 minutes. Remove vegetables and set aside.

Combine remaining 1 tablespoon soy sauce, remaining 3 tablespoons cornstarch, water, bouillon granules, and ginger; set aside.

Add pork to wok and stir-fry 4 minutes; return vegetables to wok and add bouillon mixture. Stir-fry 3 minutes or until thickened. Serve over rice.

Yield: 6 servings.

Smoked Sausage and Cabbage

1   small onion, chopped
3   tablespoons butter or margarine, melted
2   tablespoons all-purpose flour
1   cup water
$\frac{1}{2}$ teaspoon salt
$\frac{1}{4}$ teaspoon pepper
1   (2-pound) head cabbage, chopped
1   pound smoked sausage, cut into 2-inch lengths

Cook onion in butter in a large Dutch oven. Add flour, stirring until smooth. Cook 1 minute, stirring constantly. Gradually add water; cook over medium heat, stirring constantly, until thickened and bubbly. Stir in salt, pepper, and cabbage; cover, reduce heat, and simmer 5 minutes. Add sausage; cover and simmer 10 minutes. Yield: 4 servings.

LOUISE WILLIAMSON, Albany, Ga.

Oriental Lamb Chops

6   ($\frac{1}{2}$-inch-thick) lamb shoulder chops (about 2$\frac{1}{2}$ pounds)
$\frac{1}{2}$ cup soy sauce
$\frac{1}{2}$ cup water
1   clove garlic, minced

Arrange lamb chops in a large, shallow dish. Combine remaining ingredients; pour over chops. Cover; refrigerate 4 hours. Remove from marinade; discard marinade. Place on lightly greased rack in broiler pan. Broil 4 inches from heat (with electric oven door partially opened) 9 minutes; turn chops and broil 5 minutes. Yield: 6 servings.

TERESA COX, Caney, Ky.

Lamb Kabob Dinner

1½ pounds boneless lamb, cut into 1¼-inch cubes
1   cup vegetable oil
⅔   cup lemon juice
2   cloves garlic, crushed
2   teaspoons salt
½   teaspoon coarsely ground pepper
2   teaspoons dried whole dillweed
2   ears fresh corn, cut into 2-inch pieces
8   small tomatoes
16 pimiento-stuffed olives

Place lamb in a large shallow dish. Combine oil and next 5 ingredients. Pour half of mixture over lamb; cover and refrigerate at least 4 hours, stirring occasionally. Set remaining marinade aside.

Remove meat from marinade, discarding marinade; place lamb on skewers. Place corn on a separate skewer. Alternate tomatoes and olives on additional skewers.

Cook lamb without grill lid over medium coals (300° to 350°) 20 minutes, turning and basting frequently with reserved marinade. After 5 minutes, add remaining vegetable skewers; grill 15 minutes, turning and basting frequently with marinade.

Yield: 4 servings.

Note: You may substitute 1½ pounds boneless pork, cut into 1¼-inch cubes, for lamb.

Catfish With Garden Relish

2 ears fresh corn
1 tomato, chopped
1 green bell pepper, chopped
½ cup Italian salad dressing
3 tablespoons lemon juice
1 tablespoon butter or margarine, melted
4 (6-ounce) catfish fillets
2 teaspoons lemon-pepper seasoning

Cut corn from cob and place in a 1-quart baking dish. Cover tightly with heavy-duty plastic wrap; fold back a small edge of wrap to allow steam to escape. Microwave at HIGH 4 to 5 minutes or until crisp-tender; drain.

Combine corn, tomato, bell pepper, and salad dressing; refrigerate 2 hours.

Combine lemon juice and butter; brush over fillets. Arrange in a 11- x 7- x 1½-inch baking dish, placing thicker portions of fish toward outside edges of dish. Sprinkle with lemon-pepper seasoning.

Cover with plastic wrap, folding back a small edge of wrap to allow steam to escape. Microwave at MEDIUM HIGH (70% power) 10 to 12 minutes or until fish flakes easily when tested with a fork, giving dish a half-turn after 5 minutes.

Let stand, covered, 3 to 5 minutes.

Transfer fish to a plate or serving platter. Spoon vegetable mixture on top of fish.

Yield: 4 servings.

Catfish Meuniere

1 large egg, lightly beaten
¼ cup milk
½ cup all-purpose flour
½ teaspoon salt
½ teaspoon ground red pepper
4 catfish fillets (about 1½ pounds)
½ cup butter or margarine, divided
¼ cup vegetable oil
2 tablespoons chopped fresh parsley
2 tablespoons lemon juice
½ teaspoon Worcestershire sauce
Garnishes: parsley sprigs, lemon wedges

Combine egg and milk; set aside. Combine flour, salt, and red pepper. Dip fillets in egg mixture and dredge in flour mixture.

Melt ¼ cup butter in a large nonstick skillet over medium heat. Add vegetable oil; increase heat to medium-high.

Cook fillets about 4 minutes on each side or until fish flakes easily when tested with a fork. Drain on paper towels.

Melt remaining ¼ cup butter in a small saucepan; stir in parsley, lemon juice, and Worcestershire sauce. Arrange fillets on a platter and spoon butter mixture over fillets. Garnish, if desired.

Yield: 4 servings.

Chilled Salmon With Sour Cream Topping

1   (15½-ounce) can salmon, drained
½   cup sour cream
2   tablespoons chopped green onions
1   teaspoon prepared mustard
½   teaspoon lemon juice
¼   teaspoon dried dillweed
Lettuce leaves
Garnish: capers

Remove skin and bones from salmon; discard. Chill salmon. Combine sour cream and next 4 ingredients; chill.

Spoon salmon evenly onto lettuce-lined salad plates; top with sour cream mixture.

Garnish if desired. Serve immediately.

Yield: 4 servings.

WILLINE G. BELL, Daleville, Ala.

> *"A good meal makes a man feel more charitable toward the whole world than any sermon."*
>
> *ARTHUR PENDENYS*

Grilled Trout

8   (12-ounce) trout
½   cup butter or margarine, melted
3   tablespoons lemon juice
1   tablespoon plus 1 teaspoon dried parsley flakes, divided
12 lemon slices, cut in half

Dress trout by removing heads and fins.

Combine butter and lemon juice. Brush cavity of each fish with butter mixture, reserving remainder. Sprinkle cavity of each with ¼ teaspoon parsley and place 3 lemon slices in each.

Close cavities; brush outside of fish with reserved butter mixture. Sprinkle each with ¼ teaspoon parsley flakes.

Wrap trout individually in heavy-duty aluminum foil, folding edges to seal securely. Pierce foil packages several times with a wooden pick.

Cook without grill lid over hot coals (400° to 500°) 18 to 20 minutes or until fish flakes easily, turning once.

Remove from grill, unwrap, and transfer to a serving platter. Yield: 8 servings.

GERALD LEFTWICH, Sparta, N.C.

Herb-and-Mushroom Doves

3 tablespoons butter or margarine
½ teaspoon poultry seasoning
½ teaspoon dried thyme
12 whole dove breasts
¼ teaspoon salt
¼ teaspoon pepper
8 slices bacon, each cut into 3 pieces
½ pound fresh mushrooms, sliced
1 tablespoon finely chopped onion
1 tablespoon butter or margarine, melted
⅛ teaspoon garlic salt

Combine first 3 ingredients in a small saucepan; cook over medium heat until butter starts to brown. Set aside.

Sprinkle dove breasts with salt and pepper; brush with butter mixture. Place breasts, meaty side up, in a 13- x 9- x 2-inch pan and top each with 2 pieces of bacon.

Bake, uncovered, at 450° for 20 to 25 minutes or until tender.

Cook mushrooms and onion in 1 tablespoon melted butter in a skillet over medium-high heat, stirring constantly, until onion is tender; stir in garlic salt.

Transfer vegetables with a slotted spoon to a serving platter and top with doves.

Yield: 4 to 6 servings.

PATRICIA P. SANDLIN, Verbena, Ala.

Roast Pheasant

1   (3-pound) pheasant, cleaned
1   clove garlic, crushed
¼   teaspoon salt
¼   teaspoon pepper
1   bay leaf
¼   cup loosely packed celery leaves
2   slices lemon
4   slices bacon, uncooked
½   cup butter or margarine, melted
1   medium onion, sliced
2   (4-ounce) cans sliced mushrooms, undrained
1   cup chicken broth
Hot cooked brown or wild rice
Garnishes: celery leaves, lemon slices

Rinse pheasant in cold water; pat dry. Rub breast cavity with garlic; sprinkle with salt and pepper. Place bay leaf and next 2 ingredients in cavity. Lift wingtips up and over back and tuck under pheasant.

Place pheasant, breast side up, in a 13- x 9- x 2-inch pan. Place 4 slices bacon across pheasant. Cover with a double thickness of cheesecloth.

Brush butter over pheasant, coating cheesecloth. Add onion, mushrooms, and chicken broth to pan.

Bake at 350° for 3 hours or until a meat thermometer registers 185°, basting often with broth mixture.

Carefully remove cheesecloth and bacon; place pheasant on a platter. Spoon rice around pheasant; top with mushrooms and onion. Garnish, if desired.

Yield: 2 to 3 servings.

ELSIE HOFFMEYER, Wellsville, Mo.

Quail With Grapes and Almonds

1/2   **cup all-purpose flour**
1/2   **teaspoon salt**
1/4   **teaspoon pepper**
8   **quail, cleaned**
1/3   **cup butter or margarine**
1   **cup water**
1/4   **cup white wine**
Hot cooked wild rice
1   **cup seedless green grapes**
Garnishes: sliced almonds, toasted; orange slices

Combine flour, salt, and pepper; dredge quail in flour mixture. Melt butter in a large, heavy skillet; add quail and brown on both sides.

Add water and wine; cover, reduce heat, and simmer 15 minutes. Arrange quail over rice, reserving pan drippings.

Add grapes to pan drippings; cook over low heat until heated thoroughly.

Spoon sauce and grapes over quail. Garnish, if desired. Yield: 4 servings.

MARY EGLAND, Ransom, Ill.

> *"Kissing don't last; cookery do."*
> *GEORGE MEREDITH*

Quail Casserole

12   quail, dressed
½   teaspoon salt
½   teaspoon pepper
3   tablespoons butter or margarine
1   cup sliced carrots
½   cup sliced fresh mushrooms
2½ tablespoons dried onion soup mix
1   cup long-grain rice, uncooked
1   (10¾-ounce) can cream of mushroom soup,
      undiluted
1⅓ cups water
1   small onion, sliced
6   green bell pepper rings

Sprinkle quail with salt and pepper. Melt butter in skillet; add quail 6 at a time. Cook until browned on both sides. Remove quail and place in a lightly greased 13- x 9- x 2-inch baking dish.

Combine carrots and next 5 ingredients; spoon over quail.

Arrange onion slices and pepper rings on top of rice mixture. Cover and bake at 350° for 1½ hours. Let stand 10 minutes before serving. Yield: 6 servings.

CARLA KACIR, Rogers, Tex.

Marinated Venison Roast

1   (3- to 4-pound) venison roast
2   cloves garlic, minced
2   tablespoons vegetable oil
1   cup cola-flavored beverage
1¼ teaspoons salt
¼   teaspoon dry mustard
¼   teaspoon pepper
1   tablespoon white vinegar
2   tablespoons soy sauce
2   tablespoons catsup

Place roast in a shallow baking dish; set aside.

Cook garlic in oil in a saucepan over medium heat, stirring constantly, until tender. Stir in beverage and remaining ingredients. Pour over roast. Cover and refrigerate 8 hours, turning meat occasionally.

Remove roast from marinade, reserving marinade; place on a large piece of heavy-duty aluminum foil. Bring edges of foil up around roast, leaving top open. Pour marinade over roast.

Bake at 325° for 2½ hours or until a meat thermometer registers 170°, basting every 45 minutes. Yield: 10 to 12 servings.

MRS. CURTIS COPE, Byrdstown, Tenn.

Stir-Fried Venison

1   pound venison steak or tenderloin
1   tablespoon cornstarch
2   tablespoons soy sauce
1   tablespoon dry sherry
1   tablespoon sesame oil
¼   cup vegetable oil
1   tablespoon finely chopped fresh gingerroot
1   cup thinly sliced fresh broccoli
½   cup red bell pepper strips
½   teaspoon salt
1   teaspoon sugar
1   tablespoon soy sauce
1   tablespoon sliced green onions
Hot cooked rice

Partially freeze steaks; slice diagonally across grain into 2- x ½-inch strips. Sprinkle cornstarch over meat and toss gently. Stir in 2 tablespoons soy sauce and next 2 ingredients.

Pour vegetable oil into a wok or heavy skillet; heat at medium high (325°) for 1 minute. Add gingerroot and stir-fry 1 minute. Add meat and stir-fry until steak browns; remove from wok. Add broccoli and pepper; stir-fry 1 minute.

Add meat, salt, sugar, and 1 tablespoon soy sauce. Stir-fry until thoroughly heated. Stir in green onions. Serve with rice.

Yield: 4 servings.

LINDA D. WAGNER, Boneville, Ga.

Venison Chili

3   tablespoons cornstarch
3   tablespoons chili powder
1   teaspoon seasoned salt
1   teaspoon sugar
½ to 1 teaspoon cumin
1   teaspoon garlic powder
1   teaspoon dried oregano
½   teaspoon dried thyme
Pinch of dried basil
2   pounds ground venison
1   medium onion, chopped
1   (8-ounce) can tomato sauce
1   (15½-ounce) can chili beans, undrained
2¾ to 3¾ cups water

Combine first 9 ingredients; set aside.

Combine venison and onion in a Dutch oven. Cook over medium heat until venison is browned, stirring until it crumbles. Drain.

Add cornstarch mixture, stirring until well blended. Stir in tomato sauce, beans, and 2¾ cups water.

Bring to a boil; cover, reduce heat, and simmer 30 minutes, stirring occasionally. Add water, if needed, to reach desired consistency. Yield: 7 cups.

LOUISE FORD, Junction City, Ark.

Preservation

Pickling & Relishes

PROGRESSIVE FARMER
JUNE 1920

PICKLING CUCUMBERS

Clip cucumbers from vine, leaving a short stem. Wash if sandy; put in a layer of salt and a layer of cucumbers until well packed. They will make brine. Drain brine off, leaving well covered in dry salt. Soak before pickling.

PROGRESSIVE FARMER
OCTOBER 1943

PEAR RELISH

Wash and peel 2 dozen pears; remove cores. Put through food chopper to make 12 cups of ground pears. Wash and seed 6 green bell peppers and 6 red bell peppers. Peel 8 onions; grind with peppers. Mix onions and peppers with pears, 3 cups sugar, 1 quart vinegar, 2 tablespoons celery seeds, and ¼ teaspoon salt. Cook about 45 minutes. Seal hot.

❖

Just Ripe for Pickling

When you pull out those tried-and-true family pickling recipes, be sure they are up to date with current canning safety guidelines.

A Few Tips To Remember

- Acidity of vinegar should be 5%. This is indicated on the label.

- After placing food in jars, remove air bubbles with a rubber spatula. Metal utensils may scratch glass, leading to later breakage.

- Wipe jar rims clean before putting on lids and bands.

- Don't tighten bands with all your strength; a snug fit is adequate and will create the proper seal.

- Most important, process jars in a boiling-water bath for the prescribed amount of time. Processing helps protect the product from spoilage.

Mixed Vegetables Pickles

1 cup pickling salt
4 quarts cold water
1 quart sliced pickling cucumbers ($\frac{1}{2}$-inch slices)
1 quart green tomato wedges
3 cups cauliflower flowerets
2 cups small boiling onions, peeled
3 medium-size green bell peppers, coarsely chopped
3 medium-size sweet red bell peppers, coarsely
     chopped
1$\frac{1}{2}$ cups sugar
3 tablespoons mustard seed
1 tablespoon ground turmeric
5 cups white vinegar (5% acidity)
$\frac{1}{2}$ cup water

Dissolve salt in water; pour over vegetables in a large crock or plastic container. Cover and let stand in a cool place 12 to 18 hours. Drain and rinse well.

Combine sugar and remaining ingredients in a 10-quart Dutch oven; bring to a boil and boil 3 minutes. Add vegetables; reduce heat. Simmer until heated.

Pack hot vegetables into hot jars, leaving $\frac{1}{2}$ inch of headspace. Cover with hot liquid, leaving $\frac{1}{2}$ inch of headspace. Remove air bubbles; wipe jar rims. Cover at once with metal lids and screw on bands. Process in boiling-water bath 15 minutes. Yield: 8 pints.

Okra Pickles

3½ pounds small okra pods
7   cloves garlic
⅓   cup pickling salt
3   small fresh hot peppers
2   teaspoons dillseeds
1   quart water
2   cups white vinegar (5% acidity)

Pack okra tightly into hot jars, leaving ½ inch of headspace; place a garlic clove in each jar.

Combine salt and remaining ingredients in a saucepan; bring to a boil. Pour boiling vinegar mixture over okra, leaving ½ inch of headspace. Remove air bubbles; wipe jar rims. Cover at once with metal lids and screw on bands. Process in boiling-water bath 10 minutes. Yield: 7 pints.

Hot Pepper Relish

6   red bell peppers, seeded and coarsely shredded
6   green bell peppers, seeded and coarsely shredded
6   medium onions, minced
2 to 4 jalapeño peppers, chopped
1   cup sugar
1   tablespoon pickling salt
1   tablespoon mustard seeds
2   teaspoons celery seeds
2   cups cider vinegar (5% acidity)
⅓   cup hot sauce

Combine all ingredients in a large Dutch oven; bring to a boil. Reduce heat to medium. Cook, uncovered, 30 minutes, stirring occasionally. Quickly pack hot mixture into hot jars, leaving ½ inch of headspace. Remove air bubbles; cover and process as above. Yield: 7 pints.

Salads
& Dressings

VINTAGE RECIPES

PROGRESSIVE FARMER
APRIL 1929

CARROT RELISH SALAD

Mix 1 cup grated carrots with 2 cups diced celery and 2 cups diced cabbage. Moisten well with French dressing and serve cold with mayonnaise dressing and a few chopped nuts sprinkled over the top.

PROGRESSIVE FARMER
AUGUST 1942

GRAPE-LIME SALAD

Dissolve 1 package lime-flavored gelatin in boiling water. Drain 1 can white, seedless spiced grapes, reserving juice. Add enough water to make 1 cup of liquid. Stir into gelatin mixture. Add grapes; pour into individual molds. Cover and chill 8 hours. Yield: 8 servings.

Mixed Green Salad

¼ cup plus 2 tablespoons vegetable oil
3 tablespoons tarragon wine vinegar
3 tablespoons sugar
¼ teaspoon salt
⅛ teaspoon pepper
⅛ teaspoon hot sauce
6 cups mixed salad greens, torn in bite-size pieces
½ small purple onion, sliced
½ cup sliced almonds, toasted

Combine first 6 ingredients in a jar. Cover tightly, shake, and chill. Combine greens and remaining ingredients in a large bowl. Shake dressing, pour over salad, and toss. Yield: 6 servings.

Confetti Salad Dressing

1 cup vegetable oil
1 cup white vinegar
1 cup sugar
1 large green bell pepper, finely chopped
½ cup chopped green onion
1 (2-ounce) jar diced pimiento, drained
3 tablespoons prepared mustard
3 tablespoons Worcestershire sauce
1 teaspoon salt

Combine all ingredients in a jar; cover tightly and shake vigorously. Chill. Shake before serving. Yield: 3¾ cups.

MRS. LOUIS ELLIS, Lexington, Ky.

Creamy Cheese Dressing

1½ cups mayonnaise
¼ cup freshly grated Parmesan cheese
¼ cup grated Romano cheese
¼ cup milk
1½ tablespoons lemon juice
½ teaspoon freshly grated pepper
1 clove garlic, crushed

Combine all ingredients; cover and chill. Yield: 2 cups.

MARIE GREINER, Baltimore, Md.

Marinated Corn Salad

6 medium ears fresh corn
¾ cup chopped celery
½ cup chopped green bell pepper
½ cup canned red kidney beans, drained
½ cup chopped onion
1 (2-ounce) jar diced pimiento, drained
½ cup vegetable oil
½ cup white vinegar
1 teaspoon pepper
¾ teaspoon salt

Remove husks and silks from corn. Cook corn in boiling water to cover 10 minutes. Drain; cool to touch. Cut corn from cobs.

Combine corn and next 5 ingredients in a bowl; set aside.

Combine oil and remaining ingredients in a saucepan; bring to a boil and pour over vegetables. Stir well; cover and chill at least 8 hours. Serve with a slotted spoon. Yield: 8 to 10 servings.

MINNIE L. EAVES, Versailles, Ky.

Cucumber and Purple Onion Salad

3   medium cucumbers, sliced
1   medium purple onion, sliced and separated
        into rings
1   (8-ounce) carton sour cream
$\frac{1}{2}$ teaspoon white vinegar
$\frac{1}{8}$ teaspoon salt
$\frac{1}{8}$ teaspoon pepper

Arrange cucumber slices and onion rings in a large bowl; chill several hours.

Combine remaining ingredients; chill several hours. Stir before serving over salad. Yield: 8 servings.

PEGGY FOWLER REVELS, Woodruff, S.C.

Spicy French Dressing

$\frac{2}{3}$ cup sugar
$\frac{1}{2}$ cup white vinegar
1   cup vegetable oil
1   cup catsup
2   tablespoons minced onion
1   tablespoon prepared mustard
1   tablespoon Worcestershire sauce
1   teaspoon chili powder
1   teaspoon seasoned salt

Combine sugar and vinegar in a small saucepan; bring to a boil and cook until sugar dissolves.

Combine oil, remaining ingredients, and vinegar mixture in container of an electric blender; process 3 minutes. Cover and chill. Yield: $2\frac{3}{4}$ cups.

ANN C. AYLER, North, Va.

Spinach Salad

1   pound fresh spinach
1   (16-ounce) can bean sprouts, drained
1   (8-ounce) can water chestnuts, drained
3   hard-cooked eggs, sliced
6   slices bacon, cooked and crumbled
½   cup vegetable oil
¼   cup catsup
2   tablespoons white vinegar
⅓   cup sugar
Dash of salt
¼   cup chopped onion
1½ teaspoons Worcestershire sauce

Remove stems from spinach; wash leaves thoroughly and pat dry. Tear into bite-size pieces. Layer half each of spinach, bean sprouts, water chestnuts, eggs, and bacon in a large bowl. Repeat layers.

Combine oil and remaining ingredients in a jar; cover tightly and shake vigorously. Chill. Pour over spinach mixture just before serving.

Yield: 6 to 8 servings.

> *" You need to have the soul of a rabbit to eat lettuce as it is usually served — green leaves slightly lubricated with oil and flavored with vinegar. A salad is only a background; it needs embroidering."*
>
> *PAUL REBOUX*

Herbed Tomato Salad

6   tomatoes, cut into wedges
1   yellow bell pepper, cut into strips
1   red bell pepper, cut into strips
1   green bell pepper, cut into strips
1   medium-size purple onion, sliced and separated
        into rings
½   cup vegetable oil
¼   cup white vinegar
¼   cup chopped fresh parsley
¼   cup sliced green onions
¾   teaspoon fresh basil or ¼ teaspoon dried basil
¾   teaspoon fresh marjoram or ¼ teaspoon dried
        marjoram
½   teaspoon salt
¼   teaspoon pepper
Lettuce leaves

Place first 5 ingredients in a 13- x 9- x 2-inch dish; set aside.

Combine oil and next 7 ingredients in a jar; cover tightly and shake vigorously. Drizzle over vegetables; toss gently. Cover and chill at least 3 hours.

Drain vegetables and serve on a lettuce-lined platter. Serve immediately. Yield: 8 servings.

FRANCES MYERS, Apache, Okla.

Hot German Potato Salad

3 pounds red potatoes, peeled
6 slices bacon
¾ cup chopped onion
2 tablespoons all-purpose flour
1½ tablespoons sugar
1 teaspoon salt
½ teaspoon celery seeds
Dash of pepper
¾ cup water
⅓ cup white vinegar

Cook potatoes in boiling, salted water 30 minutes or until tender. Drain and slice.

Cook bacon in a large skillet until crisp. Remove bacon; crumble and set aside. Add onion to bacon drippings; cook until tender. Stir in flour and next 4 ingredients; cook over low heat 1 minute. Remove from heat; stir in water and vinegar. Bring to a boil and cook 1 minute. Add potatoes and bacon; stir gently until thoroughly heated. Yield: 8 servings.

MRS. GARY FERGUSON, Dallas, Tex.

Cauliflower Salad

1 head cauliflower, cut into flowerets
4 ounces processed cheese, cut in ½-inch cubes
½ cup chopped green bell pepper
½ cup chopped celery
½ cup sliced pimiento-stuffed olives, drained
½ cup mayonnaise

Combine first 5 ingredients in a large bowl. Add mayonnaise; toss gently. Yield: 6 servings.

KAY MEARES, Lamesa, Tex.

Layered Garden Pasta Salad

1   (8-ounce) package macaroni shells
½   cup sliced green onions
¼   cup imitation bacon bits, divided
4   cups torn lettuce (about ½ head)
1   medium zucchini, sliced
1   cup sliced cauliflower flowerets
1   cup broccoli flowerets
1   cup mayonnaise or salad dressing
¼   cup lemon juice
2   tablespoons grated Parmesan cheese
1   teaspoon sugar
½   teaspoon garlic powder
Garnish: 2 medium tomatoes, cut into wedges

Cook macaroni according to package directions; drain and rinse with cold water. Drain.

Combine macaroni, green onions, and 2 tablespoons bacon bits.

Layer lettuce, macaroni mixture, zucchini, cauliflower, and broccoli in a 3½-quart salad bowl.

Combine mayonnaise and next 4 ingredients. Spread over top of salad, sealing to edge of bowl. Cover and chill at least 2 hours.

Sprinkle with remaining 2 tablespoons bacon bits just before serving. Garnish, if desired.

Toss to serve. Yield 10 to 12 servings.

"Everything you see I owe to spaghetti."
SOPHIA LOREN

Fruited Coleslaw

½ cup chopped, unpeeled apple
1   teaspoon lemon juice
1½ cups shredded cabbage
¼ cup drained pineapple tidbits
2   tablespoons raisins
¼ cup mayonnaise
2   teaspoons lemon juice
¾ teaspoon celery seeds
½ teaspoon sugar
½ teaspoon prepared mustard

Toss apple with 1 teaspoon lemon juice in a medium bowl. Add cabbage, pineapple, and raisins; set aside.

Combine mayonnaise and remaining ingredients. Pour over cabbage mixture; toss gently. Chill 1 to 2 hours. Yield: 4 servings.

LIBBY WINSTEAD, Nashville, Tenn.

Honey Fruit Salad

1   (15¼-ounce) can pineapple chunks, undrained
2   medium oranges, peeled and sectioned
1   large apple, cored and diced
1   banana, sliced
½ cup chopped pecans
½ cup orange juice
¼ cup honey
1   tablespoon lemon juice

Combine first 5 ingredients in a large bowl; set aside. Combine remaining ingredients; pour over fruit mixture, stirring gently. Chill. Yield: 6 servings.

MRS. JACK POYNOR, Fayetteville, Ark.

Fresh Cranberry Salad

4   cups fresh cranberries
1   large orange, unpeeled, seeded, and quartered
1   cup sugar
1   (3-ounce) package lemon-flavored gelatin
1   envelope unflavored gelatin
1   cup boiling water
1   (15-ounce) can crushed pineapple, undrained
1   cup chopped pecans
½   cup finely chopped celery
Lettuce leaves

Combine cranberries, orange, and sugar; cover and chill 1 hour.

Dissolve gelatin in water; gently stir in cranberry mixture, pineapple, pecans, and celery. Spoon mixture into a 5-cup mold; chill until firm. Unmold on lettuce-lined serving plate. Yield: 8 servings.

MRS. LEWIS SELF, Sylvania, Ga.

> *"At a dinner party, one should eat wisely but not too well and talk well but not too wisely."*
>
> W. SOMERSET MAUGHAM

Soups & Sandwiches

VINTAGE RECIPES

PROGRESSIVE FARMER
AUGUST 1942

SPLIT PEA OR BEAN SOUP

Wash 1 pint of split peas or beans in the kettle. Add 2 pounds of beef or ham, ½ tablespoon salt, and sufficient water to cover all; set over fire.

As soon as it begins to boil, add a handful of celery and 1 onion. Cook 20 minutes; place the kettle in the cooker and cover quickly.

Three hours later, run the soup through a sieve into a saucepan and return it to the fire. Melt 1 tablespoon butter, add 1 tablespoon flour and stir 2 minutes. Add it to the soup, cook a few minutes, add the necessary salt and 1 tablespoon each of fine chopped parsley and fine chopped celery. Serve with small croutons.

Chicken-Vegetable Soup

1   (3- to 3½-pound) broiler-fryer
2   quarts water
1   teaspoon salt
2   (10-ounce) packages frozen mixed vegetables
1   large potato, peeled and chopped
1   (16-ounce) can tomatoes, undrained and chopped
1   (10½-ounce) can beef broth, undiluted
½   cup long-grain rice, uncooked
1   stalk celery, chopped
1   tablespoon chopped onion
¼ to ½ teaspoon pepper
¼ to ½ teaspoon poultry seasoning
2   tablespoons cornstarch
¼   cup water

Place chicken in a Dutch oven; add water and salt. Bring to a boil; cover, reduce heat, and simmer 45 minutes or until tender. Remove chicken, reserving broth in Dutch oven. Skin and bone chicken, cutting meat into bite-size pieces; set aside.

Bring broth to a boil; add frozen vegetables and next 8 ingredients. Bring to a boil; reduce heat and simmer 1 hour.

Combine cornstarch and ¼ cup water; stir into soup mixture. Add chicken and bring to a boil. Boil 1 minute. Yield: 4 quarts.

MRS. T. JASPER LOWE, Jackson, Miss.

"Only the pure in heart can make a good soup."
LUDWIG VON BEETHOVEN

Fresh Corn Chowder

3   cups cut fresh corn (about 2 pounds)
1½ cups chopped onion
⅓   cup butter or margarine, melted
⅓   cup all-purpose flour
½   teaspoon ground cumin
½   teaspoon dried marjoram
3   cups chicken broth
½   cup Chablis or other dry white wine
½   teaspoon ground nutmeg
2   cups whipping cream
½   cup diced green bell pepper
1½ cups shredded Monterey Jack cheese
2   tablespoons chopped fresh parsley
½   teaspoon salt
¼   teaspoon Worcestershire sauce
⅛   teaspoon hot sauce

Cook corn and onion in butter in a Dutch oven over medium heat, stirring constantly, 3 to 5 minutes. Add flour, cumin, and marjoram; cook 1 minute, stirring constantly.

Add chicken broth and wine; cook, stirring constantly, until mixture thickens. Add nutmeg, cream, and pepper; simmer 10 minutes. Stir in cheese and remaining ingredients; cook until cheese melts.

Yield: 9 cups.

FRANCES CHRISTOPHER, Iron Station, N.C.

Red Bean Soup

1   pound hot smoked sausage, sliced
1½ quarts water
2   (15-ounce) cans red kidney beans, undrained
1   (15-ounce) can tomato sauce
1   medium onion, chopped
1   large potato, peeled and chopped
2   carrots, sliced
1   stalk celery, chopped
2   cloves garlic, minced
⅛   teaspoon salt
⅛   teaspoon pepper
⅛   teaspoon paprika
½   cup macaroni, uncooked
½   small head cabbage, thinly sliced
2   tablespoons lemon juice

Cook sausage in a large Dutch oven until browned; drain. Return sausage to Dutch oven and add water and next 10 ingredients. Bring to a boil; reduce heat and simmer, uncovered, 1½ hours. Stir in macaroni, cabbage, and lemon juice; cook 30 minutes. Yield: about 3½ quarts.

BRENDA POGUE, Fredericktown, Mo.

> *"One of the pleasantest of all emotions is to know that I, with my brain and my hands, have nourished my beloved few, that I have concocted a stew or a story, a rarity or a plain dish, to sustain them truly against the hungers of the world."*
>
> M.F. K. FISHER

Brunswick Stew

2   pounds beef stew meat
1   (2½- to 3-pound) broiler-fryer
2   (46-ounce) cans tomato juice
1   (32-ounce) bottle catsup
7   large potatoes, peeled and cubed (about 5
        pounds)
1   (32-ounce) package frozen whole kernel corn
2   medium onions, chopped
3   tablespoons Worcestershire sauce
1   tablespoon salt
1½ teaspoons pepper
1½ teaspoons hot sauce
½   teaspoon ground red pepper

Place beef in a Dutch oven; cover with water. Bring to a boil; cover, reduce heat, and simmer 2 hours.

Remove meat from broth, saving broth for other uses; let meat cool. Coarsely chop meat; set aside.

Place broiler-fryer in a Dutch oven; cover with water. Bring to a boil; cover, reduce heat, and simmer 1 hour. Remove chicken from broth. Cool and chop meat coarsely.

Combine 4 cups chicken broth, chopped beef and chicken, tomato juice, and remaining ingredients in a large Dutch oven.

Bring to a boil. Cover, reduce heat, and simmer 2 hours. Yield: 9 quarts.

ANGELA HUGHES WATSON, Monroeville, Ala.

Irish Stew

1½ pounds beef stew meat, cut into 1-inch cubes
2   tablespoons all-purpose flour
2   tablespoons vegetable oil
3   cups water
¼   teaspoon dried oregano
¼   teaspoon dried marjoram
1   tablespoon chili powder
½   teaspoon salt
¼ to ½ teaspoon pepper
1   teaspoon steak sauce
1   teaspoon Worcestershire sauce
1   tablespoon catsup
1   medium onion, chopped
1   medium-size green bell pepper, chopped
1   stalk celery, sliced
6   medium carrots, scraped and cut into
      2-inch lengths
6   medium potatoes, peeled and quartered
1   large rutabaga, peeled and cut into 1½-inch cubes

Dredge meat in flour; cook in hot oil in a Dutch oven over medium-high heat until meat is browned.

Add water and next 11 ingredients. Bring to a boil; cover, reduce heat, and simmer 1½ hours.

Stir in carrots and remaining ingredients; cover and simmer over low heat 30 minutes or until vegetables are tender. Yield: 6 servings.

BETTY JONES, Inola, Okla.

Quick-and-Easy Chili

1¼ pounds ground beef
1   large onion, chopped
1   (16-ounce) can whole tomatoes, undrained
    and chopped
1   (16-ounce) can pork and beans, undrained
1   (15-ounce) can kidney beans, undrained
1   (11-ounce) can zesty tomato soup, undiluted
2   tablespoons chili powder
1   teaspoon salt

Combine ground beef and onion in a Dutch oven; cook, stirring often, until meat is browned and crumbled. Drain. Add tomatoes and remaining ingredients; bring to a boil and cook 3 minutes, stirring occasionally. Yield: 2 quarts.

FRANCES M. GLEICHMANN, Baltimore, Md.

"'Here, Miss,' I says, 'what d'ye call this?' 'Soup, Sir,' she says. 'Soup? Soup? Well, blast me then!' I says, polite-like. 'Is this what I've been sailin' on for the past 50 years?'"

HENRY TREWELYAN

Tuna Burgers

1   (6½-ounce) can tuna, drained and flaked
½   cup finely chopped celery
2   tablespoons minced onion
4   (¾-ounce) slices process American cheese, diced
½   cup mayonnaise or salad dressing
6   hamburger buns

Combine first 5 ingredients. Spoon about ⅓ cup on bottom half of each hamburger bun; cover with bun tops. Wrap each sandwich in aluminum foil; bake at 350° for 18 to 20 minutes or until thoroughly heated. Yield: 6 servings.

MRS. ALLEN BAKER, Harrisonburg, Va.

Egg Salad Sandwiches

8   hard-cooked eggs, chopped
6   slices bacon, cooked and crumbled
½   cup mayonnaise or salad dressing
2   teaspoons prepared horseradish
2   teaspoons Worcestershire sauce
2   teaspoons chopped onion
¼   teaspoon salt
Sandwich bread

Combine first 7 ingredients and chill 1 hour. Spread on sandwich bread. Yield: 8 servings.

EUNICE WHITE, Savannah, Tenn.

Kentucky Hot Brown Sandwiches

¼ cup butter or margarine
¼ cup all-purpose flour
2   cups milk
2   chicken-flavored bouillon cubes
6   slices bread, toasted
12 (1-ounce) slices turkey
6   (1-ounce) slices Cheddar cheese
6   slices tomato
6   slices bacon, cooked and crumbled

Melt butter in heavy saucepan over low heat; add flour, stirring until smooth. Cook 1 minute, stirring constantly. Gradually add milk and bouillon cubes; cook over medium heat, stirring constantly, until thickened and bubbly. Set aside.

Place toast in a lightly greased 13- x 9- x 2-inch baking dish. Top each slice of bread with 2 turkey slices. Spoon white sauce over turkey. Layer cheese, tomato, and crumbled bacon over sauce. Bake at 350° for 25 minutes or until bubbly. Yield: 6 servings.

J.J. JORDAN, Louisa, Ky.

"You can find your way across the country using burger joints the way a navigator uses stars."

CHARLES KURALT

Barbecued Beef Sandwiches

1   cup chopped onion
2   tablespoons vegetable oil
1   teaspoon dry mustard
2   teaspoons paprika
⅛   teaspoon garlic powder
½   teaspoon salt
1   teaspoon pepper
Dash of ground red pepper
3   tablespoons brown sugar
3   tablespoons Worcestershire sauce
1   (6-ounce) can tomato paste
3⅓ cups chopped cooked roast beef (about ¾ pound)
6   hamburger buns

Cook onion in oil in a large skillet until tender. Stir in dry mustard and next 8 ingredients.

Simmer over low heat 20 minutes, stirring occasionally. Stir in roast beef. Serve on buns.

Yield: 6 servings.

BERTHA HUBBARD, Nathalie, Va.

"For its merit, I will knight it, and then it will be Sir-Loin."

CHARLES II

Vegetables & Side Dishes

VINTAGE RECIPES

PROGRESSIVE FARMER
JUNE 1914

BAKED CABBAGE

Cook cabbage in salted, boiling water with no fat of any kind. When it can be pierced with the fork, drain, cut up, and place in an earthen dish. Pour over this a white sauce about twice as much cabbage as sauce: 2 level tablespoons flour, same of butter, 1 cup milk; bring to boil. Sprinkle with dry seasoned or buttered bread-crumbs and bake.

PROGRESSIVE FARMER
MARCH 1920

CAULIFLOWER WITH CHEESE

Chop cauliflower and arrange on shallow baking dish. Sprinkle with grated cheese and cover with buttered breadcrumbs. Bake until brown in a hot oven.

Creamy Asparagus Casserole

1 (15-ounce) can asparagus spears, drained
2 hard-cooked eggs, sliced
1 (10¾-ounce) can cream of mushroom soup,
     undiluted
¼ cup slivered almonds, toasted
3 (⅔-ounce) slices process American cheese, cubed
1 (2-ounce) jar diced pimiento, drained
½ cup saltine cracker crumbs
1 tablespoon butter or margarine, melted

Layer half each of asparagus, egg slices, soup, and almonds in a greased 1-quart casserole; repeat layers.

Cover and bake at 350° for 15 minutes. Combine cheese, pimiento, cracker crumbs, and butter; sprinkle over casserole.

Bake, uncovered, for 10 to 15 minutes.
Yield: 4 servings.

MILDRED SHERRER, Bay City, Tex.

"Eating an artichoke is like getting to know someone really well."

WILLI HASTINGS

Lemony Green Beans

3   pounds fresh green beans
6   cups water
1½ teaspoons salt
3   small onions, sliced and separated into rings
½   cup butter or margarine, melted
⅓   cup lemon juice
1   tablespoon brown sugar

Wash beans and cut into 1½-inch pieces. Place in a Dutch oven; add water and salt. Bring to a boil; cover, reduce heat, and simmer 25 to 30 minutes, stirring occasionally. Drain.

Cook onion in butter in a large skillet over medium heat, stirring constantly until tender. Add beans, lemon juice, and brown sugar.

Cook until thoroughly heated, stirring constantly. Yield: 10 to 12 servings.

Green Beans Picante

1   tablespoon butter or margarine
2   small onions, sliced and separated into rings
2   (16-ounce) cans cut green beans, drained
¼   cup picante sauce
1   tablespoon plus 1 teaspoon diced pimiento
⅛   teaspoon lemon juice

Melt butter in a saucepan; add onion and cook until tender. Add remaining ingredients; cover and heat thoroughly. Yield: 6 servings.

VICKIE DUBOIS, Erath, La.

Calico Beans

½ pound bacon, cut into 1-inch pieces
1 medium onion, chopped
½ cup firmly packed brown sugar
¼ cup catsup
1 tablespoon Worcestershire sauce
1 (16-ounce) can butterbeans, drained
1 (16-ounce) can green beans, drained
1 (16-ounce) can kidney beans, rinsed and drained
1 (16-ounce) can pork and beans

Cook bacon in a large skillet until crisp; remove bacon, reserving 2 tablespoons drippings in skillet. Cook onion in drippings, stirring constantly until crisp-tender; stir in brown sugar and remaining ingredients. Spoon into a 13- x 9- x 2-inch baking dish. Bake, uncovered, at 350° for 20 minutes or until heated. Sprinkle with bacon. Yield: 10 to 12 servings.

Broccoli Casserole

2 (10-ounce) packages frozen broccoli spears, thawed and drained
½ cup mayonnaise or salad dressing
½ cup sour cream
3 tablespoons lemon juice
¼ teaspoon salt
¼ teaspoon ground red pepper
¼ teaspoon celery salt
2 tablespoons fine dry breadcrumbs
2 teaspoons butter or margarine

Arrange broccoli in a lightly greased 2-quart casserole. Combine mayonnaise and next 5 ingredients; spread over broccoli. Sprinkle with breadcrumbs; dot with butter. Bake, uncovered, at 300° for 20 minutes or until thoroughly heated. Yield: 6 to 8 servings.

Vegetables & Side Dishes ❖

Sunshine Carrots

2 pounds carrots, scraped and thinly sliced
1 cup water
2 tablespoons cornstarch
½ cup water
1½ cups orange juice
½ teaspoon grated fresh gingerroot

Combine carrots and 1 cup water in a saucepan; bring to a boil. Cover, reduce heat, and simmer 5 to 8 minutes or until crisp-tender; drain. Set aside and keep warm.

Combine cornstarch and ½ cup water in a small saucepan, stirring until smooth. Gradually add orange juice, stirring constantly. Add ginger; stir well. Cook over medium heat until thickened and bubbly. Add sauce to carrots. Cook over medium heat until thoroughly heated.

Yield: 6 to 8 servings.

Dilled Carrots

1½ pounds carrots, scraped and diagonally sliced
Water
1 tablespoon butter or margarine
1 teaspoon dried whole dillweed
½ teaspoon sugar
⅛ teaspoon salt

Cook carrots in 1 cup boiling water 8 minutes or until crisp-tender; drain. Combine carrots and remaining ingredients in saucepan, heating until butter melts.

Yield: 6 servings.

Garden Skillet

1	small head cauliflower, separated into flowerets
2	medium zucchini, sliced
1	medium-size green bell pepper, cut into strips
1	small onion, sliced
3	tablespoons butter or margarine, melted
2	tomatoes, peeled and cut into wedges
1	teaspoon dried basil
1	teaspoon dried oregano
¾	teaspoon salt
½	teaspoon garlic powder
¼	teaspoon pepper
3	tablespoons grated Parmesan cheese, divided

Cook first 4 ingredients in butter in a large skillet, stirring constantly, 4 to 5 minutes or until crisp-tender.

Add tomatoes, seasonings, and 2 tablespoons Parmesan cheese; cook over medium heat 1 minute, tossing gently.

Transfer to serving dish; sprinkle with remaining Parmesan cheese. Yield: 6 to 8 servings.

THELMA OLSON, Lexington, Okla.

"Training is everything. The peach was once a bitter almond; cauliflower is nothing but cabbage with a college education."

MARK TWAIN

Corn Curry

3 tablespoons butter or margarine
2 cups corn cut from cob
2 tablespoons chopped onion
2 tablespoons chopped green bell pepper
½ teaspoon curry powder
½ cup sour cream
½ teaspoon salt
⅛ teaspoon pepper

Melt butter in a skillet; add corn and next 3 ingredients. Cook over low heat, stirring occasionally, 8 to 10 minutes. Stir in sour cream, salt, and pepper; cook over low heat until thoroughly heated.
Yield: 4 servings.

VELVA ROSS, Barboursville, W.Va.

Corn Casserole

3 (17-ounce) cans whole kernel corn, drained
3 (17-ounce) cans cream-style corn
¼ cup butter or margarine
3 large eggs, lightly beaten
½ cup sweetened condensed milk
Dash of salt
¼ cup fine, dry breadcrumbs
1 tablespoon butter or margarine
Garnish: fresh parsley sprigs

Combine first 6 ingredients in a Dutch oven. Bring to a boil; reduce heat and simmer 10 minutes, stirring constantly.
Spoon into a lightly greased 13- x 9- x 2-inch baking dish. Sprinkle with breadcrumbs and dot with 1 tablespoon butter. Bake at 350° for 1 hour or until set. Garnish, if desired. Yield: 16 servings.

Baked Eggplant Napoli

½ cup chopped onion
2 tablespoons vegetable oil
1 (10¾-ounce) can tomato puree
⅔ cup water
1 tablespoon chopped fresh oregano or 1 teaspoon
    dried oregano
½ teaspoon salt
⅛ teaspoon pepper
1 (1-pound) eggplant, peeled and cut into ¼-inch
    slices
2 cups (8 ounces) shredded sharp Cheddar cheese,
    divided

Cook onion in oil in a saucepan over medium heat, stirring constantly, until tender. Add tomato puree and next 4 ingredients; bring to a boil. Reduce heat and simmer 15 minutes.

Layer half each of eggplant and tomato mixture in a lightly greased 11- x 7- x 1½-inch baking dish. Top with 1 cup cheese, remaining eggplant, and tomato mixture; cover and bake at 350° for 55 minutes.

Uncover, sprinkle with remaining cheese and bake 5 additional minutes. Yield: 6 to 8 servings.

MRS. PARKE LAGOURGUE CORY, Neosho, Mo.

> "*The destiny of nations depends upon what and how they eat.*"
>
> *JEAN-ANTHELME BRILLAT-SAVARIN*

Turnip Greens With Cornmeal Dumplings

1 **bunch turnip greens (2 pounds)**
1 **teaspoon salt**
4 **cups water**
¼ **pound salt pork**
¾ **cup plus 1 tablespoon self-rising cornmeal**
1 **large egg, lightly beaten**
¼ **cup milk**
1 **tablespoon vegetable oil**

Remove and discard stems and any discolored spots from greens. Wash thoroughly and place in a Dutch oven. Add salt and enough cold water to cover; let soak 1 hour. Rinse and drain.

Combine 4 cups water and salt pork in Dutch oven; bring to a boil. Add greens; return to a boil. Reduce heat and simmer, uncovered, 20 minutes.

Combine cornmeal and remaining ingredients, stirring until dry ingredients are moistened. Drop mixture by tablespoonfuls onto hot turnip greens; cover and simmer over medium heat 15 minutes. Yield: 6 servings.

DARLENA LEWIS, Pikeville, Tenn.

"If you can't stand the heat, get out of the kitchen."

HARRY VAUGHAN
(OFTEN USED BY HARRY S. TRUMAN.)

Okra With Corn

½ cup plus 2 tablespoons butter or margarine
2 medium-size green bell peppers, chopped
½ cup sliced green onions
1½ cups sliced fresh okra
1½ cups corn cut from cob (about 6 ears)
⅔ cup boiling water
½ teaspoon salt
⅛ teaspoon pepper

Melt butter in a large, heavy skillet; add green peppers and onions. Cook 2 minutes, stirring constantly. Add remaining ingredients; cover and simmer 10 minutes or until vegetables are tender. Yield: 8 servings.

CINDY MURPHY, Cleveland, Tenn.

Spiced Sweet Onions

3 large sweet onions
6 whole cloves
¼ teaspoon salt
3 tablespoons butter or margarine, melted
1 tablespoon brown sugar
¼ teaspoon ground nutmeg
Dash of ground red pepper
¼ cup slivered almonds, toasted

Cut onions in half crosswise and cook in boiling water 15 minutes or until almost tender. Drain well. Arrange, cut side up, in an 11- x 7- x 1½-inch baking dish. Insert a whole clove in center of each onion half and sprinkle with salt.

Combine butter and next 3 ingredients; drizzle over onions. Cover and bake at 325° for 45 minutes or until tender. Sprinkle with almonds. Yield: 6 servings.

BOBBIE MAE COOLEY, Bowen, Ill.

Peppery Potato Medley

¼ cup vegetable oil
6 large potatoes, cut into ¼-inch slices (about
    3 pounds)
1 large onion, thinly sliced
1 green bell pepper, thinly sliced
1 clove garlic, chopped
4 jalapeño peppers, seeded and thinly sliced
1 medium zucchini or yellow squash, thinly sliced
2 tablespoons sugar
1 teaspoon salt
¼ teaspoon pepper

Cook potatoes and next 4 ingredients in oil in a Dutch oven over medium heat, stirring occasionally, until potatoes are almost tender. Add squash and sprinkle with sugar, salt, and pepper.

Cover and cook 5 to 7 minutes or until potatoes are tender, stirring occasionally. Yield: 8 servings.

MRS. ELMER DANIELS, Alanreed, Tex.

> *"Pray for peace and grace and spiritual food, for wisdom and guidance, for all these are good, but don't forget the potatoes."*
>
> *J.T. PETTEE*

Sweet Potato Casserole

1 (15¼-ounce) can unsweetened pineapple chunks,
   undrained
2 cups firmly packed brown sugar
3 tablespoons cornstarch
½ cup butter or margarine
5 large sweet potatoes, cooked, peeled, and mashed

Drain pineapple, reserving juice. Set pineapple aside. Add enough water to juice to make 2 cups liquid.

Combine brown sugar and cornstarch in a saucepan; gradually add pineapple juice, stirring well. Add butter and cook over medium heat until smooth and thickened, stirring constantly.

Spoon potatoes in mounds in a lightly greased 13- x 9- x 2-inch baking dish; pour sauce over potatoes. Top with pineapple. Bake at 350° for 15 to 20 minutes or until bubbly.

Yield: 12 to 15 servings.

"Four decades of cooking have taught me a few do's and don'ts. One of the things I do is to use herbs and spices. One of the don'ts is not to use them with a heavy hand."

MARIE PIETRI KILPATRICK

Mushroom-Stuffed Yellow Squash

4   medium-size yellow squash
¼   cup butter or margarine
½   pound fresh mushrooms, chopped
1   small onion, chopped
1   clove garlic, minced
1   cup soft breadcrumbs
½   teaspoon salt
¼   teaspoon pepper

Cook squash in boiling water to cover 8 to 10 minutes or until tender but still firm. Drain and cool slightly.

Cut each squash in half lengthwise; remove and reserve pulp, leaving the shell intact. Chop pulp and set aside.

Melt butter in a skillet; add mushrooms, onion, and garlic and cook over medium heat, stirring constantly, until tender.

Remove from heat and stir in squash pulp, breadcrumbs, salt, and pepper.

Place squash shells in a 13- x 9- x 2-inch baking dish.

Spoon squash mixture into shells. Bake at 350° for 15 minutes. Yield: 4 servings.

MRS. D. M. SMITH, Gainesville, Fla.

Zucchini Creole

1¾ pounds zucchini, sliced
½ pound fresh mushrooms, sliced
1 large green bell pepper, cut into thin strips
1 large onion, cut into thin strips
1 clove garlic, minced
2 tablespoons chopped fresh basil or 2 teaspoons
   dried basil
1 tablespoon butter or margarine, melted
½ teaspoon sugar
½ teaspoon salt
¼ teaspoon pepper
¼ teaspoon Worcestershire sauce
2 medium tomatoes, peeled and chopped

Combine first 11 ingredients in a large skillet.
Cook over medium heat 5 minutes, stirring often. Add
tomatoes and cook 5 additional minutes or until vegetables are tender. Yield: 8 servings.

MRS. E. R. SELLARS, Oklahoma City, Okla.

> *"Cheese, milk's leap toward immortality."*
> CLIFTON FADIMAN

Baked Green Tomatoes

8   medium-size green tomatoes, peeled and cut into
     ½-inch slices
1   cup fine, dry breadcrumbs
½   cup grated Parmesan cheese
1   teaspoon salt
⅛   teaspoon pepper
3   tablespoons butter or margarine

Arrange half of tomatoes in a lightly greased 13- x 9- x 2-inch baking dish. Combine breadcrumbs and next 3 ingredients; sprinkle half of mixture over tomatoes and dot with butter.

Top with remaining tomato slices and crumb mixture. Bake at 350° for 45 to 50 minutes.

Yield: 8 to 10 servings.

MRS. F. QUESENBERRY, Fancy Gap, Va.

Cheesy Broiled Tomato

1   large tomato, halved
½   teaspoon sugar
1   tablespoon grated Parmesan cheese

Sprinkle cut side of tomato with sugar and Parmesan cheese. Broil 4 inches from heat (with electric oven door partially opened) 3 to 5 minutes or until lightly browned. Serve immediately.

Yield: 2 servings.

ADELYNE SMITH, Dunnville, Ky.

Wild Rice Dressing

2   (6-ounce) packages long-grain and wild rice mix
⅔   cup chopped onion
½   cup butter or margarine, melted
½   cup all-purpose flour
2   cups chicken broth
1   cup half-and-half
1½ teaspoons poultry seasoning
⅛   teaspoon pepper
2   (4-ounce) jars diced pimiento, drained
⅔   cup chopped fresh parsley
½   cup slivered almonds, toasted

Cook rice mix according to package directions; set aside.

Cook onion in butter in a large skillet over medium heat, stirring constantly, until tender. Add flour, stirring until smooth. Cook 1 minute, stirring constantly. Gradually add chicken broth and half-and-half; cook over medium heat, stirring constantly, until mixture is thickened and bubbly.

Stir in poultry seasoning and remaining ingredients. Add rice, mixing well. Spoon into a lightly greased 13- x 9- x 2-inch baking dish. Cover and bake at 375° for 30 minutes.

Yield: 8 to 10 servings.

Note: To make ahead, assemble casserole; cover and chill. Remove from refrigerator and let stand 30 minutes. Bake as directed.

CHARLSIE A. PARKS, New Albany, Miss.

Nassau Grits

4½ cups water
1¼ teaspoons salt
1   cup regular grits, uncooked
½   cup chopped onion
¼   cup chopped green bell pepper
1   tablespoon butter or margarine, melted
1   (16-ounce) can tomatoes, drained and chopped
¼   teaspoon pepper

Combine water and salt in a heavy saucepan; bring to a boil. Stir in grits; cover, reduce heat, and simmer 25 minutes or until water is absorbed.

Cook onion and bell pepper in butter in a large skillet over medium heat, stirring constantly, until tender; stir in grits. Add tomatoes and pepper; cook until thoroughly heated. Yield: 6 to 8 servings.

Mushroom-Pecan Rice

1   cup brown rice, uncooked
½   teaspoon ground nutmeg
1   (10¾-ounce) can cream of mushroom soup,
      undiluted
1   (4-ounce) can mushroom stems and pieces, drained
½   cup coarsely chopped pecans
2   tablespoons butter or margarine, melted

Prepare rice according to package directions, adding salt, if desired. Combine rice and next 3 ingredients in a greased 2-quart baking dish; set aside.

Cook pecans in butter in a small skillet until lightly toasted; sprinkle over rice mixture. Bake, uncovered, at 350° for 20 minues. Yield: 4 to 6 servings.

ALICE MCNAMARA, Eucha, Okla.

Safe Freezer Storage Time Chart

Baked goods
Bread ....3 months
Cakes ....3-5 months
Cookies................6 months
Pies and pastry .....2 months

Dairy
Butter ....6 months
Cheese ....4 months
Ice Cream ....1-3 months
Eggs:
whites................6 months
yolks...................8 months

Fish and shellfish
Fat fish ....3 months
Lean fish...............6 months
Shellfish................3 months

Poultry
Chicken,
whole ....3-6 months
Chicken,
pieces.................3 months
Chicken,
cooked ....1 month
Turkey ....6 months

Meat
Beef ....6-12 months
Pork....................3-6 months
Lamb.................6-9 months
Veal ....6-9 months
Ground meats...3-4 months
Ham ....1-2 months
Bacon......................1 month
Frankfurters..............1 month
Sausage.................2 months
Variety meats ....3-4 months
Leftover cooked
meat...................3 months

Vegetables and fruits
Vegetables,
commercially
frozen ....8 months
Vegetables,
home frozen....12 months
Fruits,
commercially
frozen ....12 months
Fruits,
home frozen....12 months

Equivalent Measurements

3 teaspoons = 1 tablespoon

4 tablespoons = ¼ cup

5⅓ tablespoons = ⅓ cup

8 tablespoons = ½ cup

16 tablespoons = 1 cup

2 tablespoons
(liquid) = 1 ounce

1 cup = 8 fluid ounces

2 cups = 1 pint
(16 fluid ounces)

4 cups = 1 quart

4 quarts = 1 gallon

⅛ cup = 2 tablespoons

⅓ cup = 5 tablespoons plus
1 teaspoon

⅔ cup = 10 tablespoons plus
2 teaspoons

Light Substitutes

Dairy Products and Eggs

Instead of	*Substitute*
Whole milk or 2% milk	Skim or 1% milk
Sour cream	Plain low-fat yogurt or nonfat yogurt
American or Cheddar cheese	Low-fat or 40% less fat cheeses or use half low-fat cheese and half regular
Cream cheese	Neufchâtel or light cream cheese
Creamed cottage cheese	1% low-fat cottage cheese or part-skim ricotta
Whole eggs	Egg whites or egg substitute

Meat, Fish, and Poultry

Sausage, bacon, and organ meats such as liver	Fish, poultry with all the skin removed, and lean cuts of beef, pork, lamb (Trim all meats well.)
Bacon, ham hocks, fatback for cooking vegetables	Lean ham or Canadian bacon
Bologna, salami, luncheon meats, and hot dogs	Sliced chicken or turkey breast, tuna, lean roast beef (Choose low-fat cooking methods such as broiling, stir-frying, or poaching.)

Fats, Oils, Gravies, and Sauces

Butter	Margarine made from a liquid vegetable oil (Tub and liquid margarines have less saturated fat than stick margarines.)
Butter for sauteing	Vegetables cooked in bouillon or vegetable cooking spray
Lard or vegetable shortening	Vegetable oil (When required for baking, try oil, using ⅓ less the amount of solid fat or a polyunsaturated stick margarine.)
Mayonnaise	Reduced-calorie mayonnaise or plain low-fat yogurt
Sauces made with cream	Nonfat dry milk made extra strength (½ cup milk powder to 1 cup skim milk)
Fat for greasing pans	Vegetable cooking spray

Index